W9-CEO-642

Winning Your Spurs

Winning Your Spurs

by

Elaine T. Moore

Illustrated by Paul Brown

Bramhall House   •   *New York*

COPYRIGHT 1953, 1954, BY ELAINE T. MOORE

ALL RIGHTS RESERVED. NO PART OF THIS BOOK IN EXCESS OF FIVE
HUNDRED WORDS MAY BE REPRODUCED IN ANY FORM WITHOUT
PERMISSION IN WRITING FROM THE PUBLISHER

LIBRARY OF CONGRESS CATALOG CARD NO. 54-5146

*This edition is published by Bramhall House,
a division of Clarkson N. Potter, Inc.,
by arrangement with Little, Brown and Company.*
(A)

PRINTED IN THE UNITED STATES OF AMERICA

To Roulette

Acknowledgment

The author wishes to acknowledge the kind co-operation of the American Horse Shows Association and the American Society for the Prevention of Cruelty to Animals.

All references to rules of the American Horse Shows Association are taken with the association's permission from its 1954 Rule Book.

— E.T.M.

Contents

Illustrations

ILLUSTRATIONS

PART ONE

Horsemanship

CHAPTER I

The Importance of Learning

THE FIRST really exciting day of your riding career is a day when you have ridden hard and well. Your instructor walks across the ring with a shiny new pair of spurs in his hands and gives them to you saying only, "Here. You've earned them."

This is the first sign of recognition for the countless hours you've spent working hard both on and off your horse; the hours of walk, trot and canter in circles and figure eights, and the hours you have spent in the barn, learning everything you could about horses, learning to understand them and to work with them. He may not smile as he hands you those spurs, but you know he's pleased. You know that you have accomplished a great deal, or he wouldn't have given you the spurs. It means that you've finished your apprenticeship, and you'll have more of the good horses to ride. It means that your legs are steady and don't swing any more, because your balance is finally right, so that when you wear those spurs you won't jab your horse's sides with them when he doesn't need it. It means that your hands are quiet and controlled, so that you won't be pulling on your horse's mouth at the same time you're using your spurs. It's a very exciting day!

It's a long way from the day you first mount a horse until you win those spurs, but every bit of it is worthwhile. In riding, perhaps more than in any other sport, every bit of learning is important. It not only means more fun and excitement, but more important, it is your assurance of increased safety on a horse. It enables you to master your horse in order to get the best possible performance from him and lessen the element of chance. A horse is like a very complex machine, and just as you must know about a machine before you can operate it, you must know all about your horse. This knowledge is the foundation of what we call horsemanship.

Just as the word suggests, horsemanship is simply the relationship between the horse and the rider, and the way they work together for a smooth performance. Equitation is horsemanship plus the skill of the rider to make himself look like part of the horse, so that the performance is so smooth that the rider's mastery is concealed. It is a perfect co-ordination of the body *and* temperament of the rider with the body

3

and temperament of the horse that makes the horse's obedience seem instinctive. But we must start at the very beginning.

First, you must learn to be a very good sport, for this is the basis of all sport. Sportsmanship is winning or losing with a smile, inside as well as out. But even more, it is understanding and loving your animal completely, and being humble and modest. This love and understanding of your horse is the essence of good horsemanship, because a poor sport can never learn. He cannot learn because every mistake he makes will be blamed on the horse, or the footing, or the weather, or any one of the many things which might affect his riding and performance. A good sport will realize that every mistake is his own fault, and instead of blaming something else he will blame himself, and try to correct his mistakes. If he realizes that his horse's mistakes are his own, he can improve himself and his horse. He can achieve a harmony with his horse which is the basis of horsemanship and, when he is able to achieve this harmony with any animal he mounts, it is also the final measure of his skill. Once a rider has a true understanding of his horse he will become a true horseman, not just a rider. A horseman can go on perfecting his skill indefinitely, for one never finishes learning how to ride. There is always a challenge in a new horse or a new course, and this constant challenge is one of the things that makes riding such an exciting sport.

From the moment you mount your horse it is in your hands not only to guide and direct him, but also to teach him, *either* good or bad. Your horse responds to everything you do — *or don't do* — when you are on him. You must punish him when he disobeys, and reward him when he is good. And since every rider is responsible for every mistake his horse makes, the rider is responsible to himself *and* to his horse to improve himself constantly. Your horse's reactions are a mirror of your horsemanship. Perfect horsemanship will result in a well-schooled horse, for as you improve yourself, you will also improve your horse.

To *learn* to do anything you must *do* it. This applies especially to riding. The only way to learn to ride is to spend hours in the saddle, though your work must be supervised. You should spend at least five hours in practice for every half-hour lesson. In other words, you must have lessons often enough to keep you from getting into any bad habits, but you should space these lessons far enough apart to give you time to concentrate on what you have already learned, until it becomes automatic. Once it is automatic, you can go on to the next lesson without having to think about what you have previously been taught, and yet you won't lose it. You need your whole mind free to apply to each new lesson without having to think of the one before.

Do not try to learn to ride without a competent instructor. Regardless of how many books you have read or how much you know about horses, you cannot possibly learn to ride without having someone to guide you and supervise your work. In the first place, you cannot see yourself as a whole in order to check your position.

4

Anything you are doing wrong will become progressively worse, not better, no matter how much you ride, and you will get into terrible habits which may take years to correct. In the second place, a good instructor knows how to *teach*, and drawing on years and years of experience he will be able to tell you one simple thing which will correct a particular fault without your even realizing it. He may correct your knees by adjusting your feet, or correct your back by adjusting your head. He knows just the key to each problem because he has seen so many people with the same difficulties. There is absolutely no substitute for good instruction; it is indispensable to anyone who wants to learn.

You must be sure, however, that you do get *good* instruction. Your teacher may not say much to you, but what he says will be important and will help you. A good instructor may make you do things you don't like to do and ride horses you hate, but he does it only because he wants you to learn, not to waste your time and his. A good instructor must be a good horseman, though not necessarily a magnificent rider. His job is to teach, not ride. He will be calm and stern with horses, and he will usually know just what a horse is going to do before he does it. And to benefit from his knowledge, you must pay strict attention and obey his orders without question.

Even after you have had years of instruction, however, your "hours in the saddle" are still important. Though it will take less time to master things after you have had some experience, the problems will be more difficult and less tangible. They will be problems which can only be solved by a matter of "feeling" or timing. The amount of time which it will take to "get the feel" of something will vary with each problem, each horse, and each rider, so every minute in the saddle will still count. Don't ever think that you have "learned how to ride." Even the finest riders in the country still return to their instructors periodically for help. There is always more to be learned about riding, schooling and horses.

When I had been riding for years my instructor could still present a problem which I would understand in theory, after explanation, but which I couldn't apply successfully on a horse. When I got discouraged and asked why I couldn't do it, he would only say, "Hours in the saddle," and I learned he was right. He had told me all he could tell me, I had read all I could read, but it was a matter of trying and trying, and finally it would work. Sometimes it would take hours, sometimes days, sometimes longer, but it would be worth it when I could say at last, "I've got it!" and know I wouldn't lose it.

Another very important point in learning to ride is to ride as many different horses as possible, rather than just the horses you like. In fact, you should ride the horses you *dis*like most often, because those are the horses which present the most challenge, and from which you can learn the most, because they make you work. Whenever you ride a horse you really like you are not learning, for you wouldn't like him unless you had learned how to master him. Even if you fool yourself and say you like him because he isn't easy to ride, it only means that you know what bad habits he has and they don't bother you because you know what to expect. So this is no excuse. On these horses you are just taking a pleasure ride, and such rides should not be counted among your hours of real riding. The wisest instructors, who are not afraid of displeasing their pupils but want them to learn how to ride, will find out which horses they dislike, and make them ride those horses constantly until they actually learn to like them.

There's an old sarcastic saying among horsemen, "Good horses make good riders." It means that anyone looks good on a good horse, but it takes a really good rider to ride a bad horse well. First learn to ride the lazy ones, the stubborn ones, the green ones, *then* you may ride the good ones.

No two horses are exactly the same, so you will learn something different from each one. Yet each thing you learn you will be able to apply to some other horse, some other time. The more horses you ride, the more horses you will be *able* to ride. You may ride one or two horses perfectly, but you may get on another which is actually no harder to ride, just different, and not be able to ride him at all. That is why you are often asked to change horses in horsemanship classes at shows. It shows the judge just how much experience and natural ability you have with different types of horses.

So you see, your learning will be limited only by the number of horses you ride. The more different types you ride, the wider will be your range of experience which will enable you to cope with all kinds of horses, their temperaments, and their bad habits. Just as every teacher learns from his pupils, every rider learns from his horses.

SUMMARY

There is a great deal to be learned before you have earned your spurs, for the winning of your spurs is your reward for having completed your apprenticeship. There are three steps toward learning: first, sportsmanship, for without it you cannot progress; second, hours in the saddle under the proper guidance, for this gives you feeling and timing; third, riding different horses, for your experience is limited by the number of horses you have ridden. Riding presents a constant challenge, so you can never stop learning.

CHAPTER II

Understanding Your Horse

GOOD HORSEMANSHIP is not just looking pretty on a horse, it is working well *with* a horse. You can't be a good rider without a horse. You and your horse make up a team dependent upon one another, and you must work together for a good performance. You have to know how to get the *most* out of him with the *least* effort. And to do this you must understand his temperament, understand what makes him tick.

Each horse is an individual, just as you are, and has his own definite will and personality. His temperament is made up of two basic things: first, his natural animal instincts, and second, his memory. If we can understand how these two things cause his various reactions, we can learn to expect certain things and master him more easily.

The horse's greatest instinct is fear. By knowing what he fears and why, we can avoid frightening him and endangering our own safety. He is especially afraid of anything sudden, anything which he does not understand, and anything which reminds him of unpleasant experiences he may have had. We cannot know what these past experiences were, but we do know about the basic fears which most horses share. We know that we mustn't come up behind him without warning him with a soothing voice, or he may kick out, sensing that something is going to be done to him. We mustn't suddenly raise a hand around him, for he will expect to be hit. If you want to pick up his foot you must start at his shoulder and run your hand down his leg. To get to his ears you should start at his muzzle and work upwards. Also, we mustn't shout at him suddenly, except as a punishment to make him stop kicking in his stall, or nipping at another horse, or generally misbehaving when we are working with him.

There are some fears from past experiences which are, unfortunately, fairly common. Many horses are afraid to mount a van ramp because they have either been beaten on one or have fallen off one and hurt or frightened themselves. A horse may be difficult to shoe because he has had a nail driven into the sensitive quick of his foot

7

by a careless blacksmith, or he may have been beaten while being shod. It is only natural that horses retain such fears, and we must respect them.

The only way to overcome fear is with patience. Fear must be treated with kindness, never punishment. If a horse is punished when he is already afraid, he will only become more frightened. You will build up your horse's confidence in you by avoiding this. And by understanding your horse's fears you can gain confidence in *him*.

One time on a ranch out West the wrangler brought a supposedly "saddle-broke" horse in from the range. The horse galloped wildly around the corral, eyes rolling, nostrils flared, bucking and kicking. The wrangler just stood there talking to him till he quieted down a little. When one of the dudes later asked the wrangler how he dared stay in the corral with such an awful beast, he answered, "Why, he's just a'feared, ma'am."

A horse's fear both endangers and protects us. It is dangerous only when it is unexpected, because when it is anticipated it can be avoided. There is not a horseman alive who will not use his voice or grab a few strands of a horse's tail when passing his heels. Strangely enough, a horse won't kick as long as you are holding onto his tail.

On the other hand, a horse's natural fear of humans protects us. Any horseman will stand in the path of a galloping horse in order to stop him, because he knows that a horse won't run over a person. I had one filly who would always run right up to me at a full gallop when she was in pasture, but when she was within one or two feet of me, she would put on the brakes and nearly sit down in order to stop immediately. Though she just thought it was good sport, I found it rather frightening at first, until I learned I was perfectly safe. And for the same reason, though there are so very many spills which land a rider right under a jumping horse's feet so very few riders are ever stepped on — in fact, I have never known anyone to be stepped on except, perhaps, in steeplechasing. I have had countless falls where it seemed inevitable that the horse would land right on me, yet I have never been stepped on or kicked, and have only occasionally been grazed by the hoofs. Somehow horses always manage to extend or shorten their stride or to twist in mid-air to avoid landing on the rider. It is really remarkable, and comforting!

Just as you must earn your horse's confidence, you must be confident in him, for any fear will prevent you from being able to ride well. Never be afraid of your horse, whether you are on or off him, for he will sense it and be frightened by your fear. Be wary, of course, for any animal is unpredictable. You should never go into a horse's stall when he is lying down, for instance, for he will usually try to get up the minute you come in, and horses do this so awkwardly that you may be accidentally hit by a flying foot. Don't be afraid, just be careful. And never give a horse cause to fear you, only to respect you, for you must trust one another in order to work well together.

You must also realize that the horse ranks low in intelligence, though we often think of him as being smart because of his memory. A horse can be taught many things because he can remember when he has been rewarded and when he has been punished. That is why we base our schooling methods on reward and punishment — it is by far the most successful system. And that is why we must never let a horse misbehave without being punished, for he will do anything he can get away with, and the disobedience will become greater and greater until it is almost impossible to correct.

If, for example, you dismount after riding and your horse rubs his head against you playfully, it is because the sweat under his bridle has caused his head to itch — not because he is being affectionate. If you scratched his head, it would encourage him until he nearly knocked you down each time you dismounted. Instead, you must gently but firmly slap his nose. The next time you dismount, take his bridle off as soon as possible, and dry the sweaty part of his head with your rub-rag. This way you will remove the cause of the disobedience and the need for punishment. We don't want to punish any more than we really need to, for the punishment will lose its effectiveness.

Or perhaps when you are riding along the path your horse puts his nose down to the side to grab some grass. If you let him do this, thinking it does no harm, soon he will learn to put his head down every other stride and probably succeed in dumping you in the bargain, because he will do it quickly, knowing it is wrong. Any time he tries this, you should jab the opposite side of his mouth with a quick, strong jerk on the rein, pulling his head up and away from the grass. If you are consistent with this punishment, he will associate the bite of grass with an unpleasant jab on his mouth, and he will give up trying to get the grass. Only punish your horse when he deserves it, but when you do, be *firm*. He must respect your authority.

Not only must you understand your horse, but you must make him understand you. Before you can punish him for a disobedience you must be sure that he *has* disobeyed, that you have given him a clear command which he has willfully resisted or ignored. You must first decide what you want him to do and then follow through to the finish *without hesitation*. During a moment's hesitation he will have thought of something else to do. You wouldn't run halfway across a street and then stop to decide what to do, so you shouldn't do it on a horse. Don't ask one thing, change your mind, and settle for something else. Know exactly what you want and be sure your horse knows it by a positive command. Then, if he disobeys, punish him by insisting on his finishing the task.

SUMMARY

Good horsemanship is working well with a horse by understanding his individual temperament. His actions are based on two motives: first, *animal instincts, of which the greatest is fear, both natural and acquired;* second, *memory, which is what passes for intelligence. Fear is overcome only by patience; respect his fear and teach him to have confidence in you, but do not be afraid of him. His memory gives us the basis of our schooling methods — reward and punishment. He will learn that when he disobeys he is punished, and when he is good he is rewarded. If a disobedience goes unpunished he will try it again, exaggerating it until it has become a bad habit. But always make your commands clear to him so that if he disobeys and is punished he will know* why *he is being punished.*

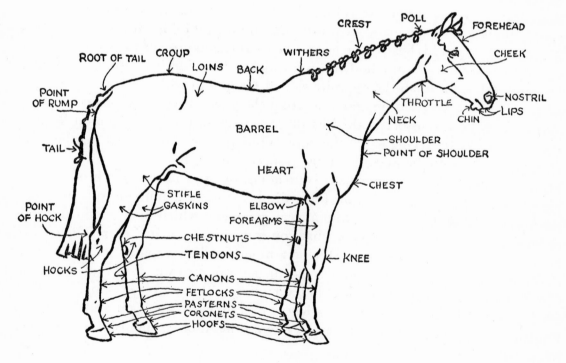

PARTS OF THE HORSE

CHAPTER III

Conformation

W E HAVE SEEN the importance of understanding the horse's temperament, but before we can achieve the perfect performance for which we strive, we should know all about his anatomy so that we can co-ordinate our own body with his. Just as it is unfair to punish a horse for reactions caused by fear or ignorance, it is unfair to punish him for what he is physically unable to do. The perfect saddle horse, for example, is the exact opposite of the perfect hunter, so it would be wrong to expect the saddle horse to be able to perform the duties of the hunter. And what is poor conformation for one person's needs might be all right for another's, and vice versa.

Conformation is simply how a horse is put together, how well proportioned he is. It is judged on how closely the horse conforms to the established standard of perfection for his type or breed, and each type of horse is bred in accordance with the function it will be expected to perform. Each horse's conformation is different, individually and as a type. There are many different breeds for many different purposes: Morgan, originally a mixture of Arab, Thoroughbred and cold blood and used as a harness horse, saddle horse, trotter, light draft horse, and jumper; Arabian, virtually the ancestor of all light breeds; Barb, similar to the Arabian and possibly an offshoot of that breed; Standard Bred, trotter; Hackney, harness horse; Palomino, saddle horse; Tennessee Walking Horse; Welsh Pony; Shetland Pony; Quarter Horse, a race horse descended from a Thoroughbred but unlike him in appearance; Belgian, Cleveland Bay, Clydesdale, Percheron, Suffolk, and Shire, all draft horses; Thoroughbred, descended from one of three foundation sires of Arab blood introduced to England around 1700, also progenitor of trotters, saddle horses and Morgans, and bred today either for speed as race horses or conformation and jumping ability as hunters; American Saddle Horse, either three-gaited or five-gaited, descended from Arabian and Thoroughbred blood. Polo ponies are a type, not a breed, and are mixtures of Thoroughbred, Arabian, Morgan, Quarter Horse or Welsh blood, or Thoroughbred mixed with Western. Western ponies are generally cold-blooded, though they sometimes

11

have Arabian or Thoroughbred blood in them. Hunters are often cold-blooded also, or a mixture of Thoroughbred and some other blood.

But breeding is only the basis for training. The saddle-horse colt, for example, is far from the saddle horse you see in the show ring. He is bred with a well-crested neck, a long back, a high-set tail. But his training will include the setting of his tail to make it stand higher, the use of a heavy curb bit to increase the arch of his neck and bring his chin in close to his chest, the use of weights on his feet to give him higher action in his gaits, and so forth. His breeding makes these things possible. They couldn't be done with a hunter.

But since the hunter-type horse is generally most useful, being able to hack, jump, show, foxhunt or travel cross-country, we should know what kind of conformation is most desirable for him. The conformation of a hunter is judged on what has proved to be the safest and most adaptable for his purposes, as well as what makes him picture-pretty for the show ring.

Unlike the gaited horse, the natural center of the hunter's weight is just behind his shoulder, where he is deep through the heart. It allows a natural carriage of his head and neck and leaves his hindquarters free for the action and power necessary

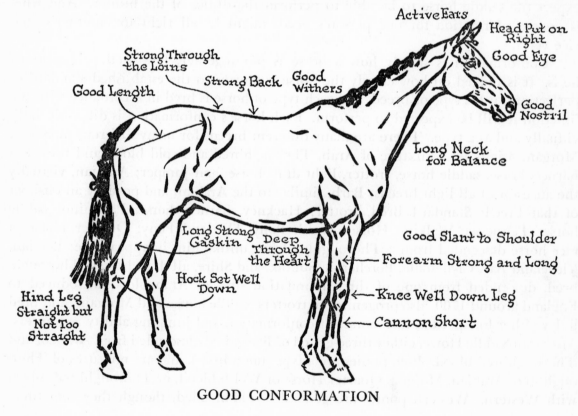

GOOD CONFORMATION

12

for his gaits and for jumping. The fact that the hunter's balance is centered on his forequarters is important in the placement of the rider's weight on his back. Behind the saddle there is no bone other than the spine to support weight. This section between the rib cage and the hips also holds the sensitive kidneys, and too much weight on this region can cause serious injury to the horse. Many horses will flinch when you mount them if you should land too heavily, though it does not necessarily mean they have particularly weak kidneys.

Perfect conformation does not mean that a horse will perform any better or be any easier to ride, but there are certain faults and unsoundnesses which make a horse less safe or less comfortable. In some cases, comfort must be sacrificed for safety. Some faults which make a horse unsafe for jumping need not be considered too seriously if he is only going to be used for hacking or to pop an occasional jump on the path. Even faults which are considered serious in the show ring, such as splints or bowed tendons, are not too important, except that allowance must be made for them when you are working a horse with these weaknesses.

The size of your horse is unimportant, also, except in relation to your own size and anatomy. Small horses are no easier to ride than large ones, nor are large ones better jumpers because of their height. If you should have short or rounded legs, a narrow, slab-sided horse will certainly be easier for you to ride than a round one. If you have long legs, you will want a large round horse, so that your legs won't hang beneath his stomach.

Below is an explanation of each of the important faults and unsoundnesses which are to be found in horses. You cannot expect to be able to judge a horse's conformation simply from reading about it, but you should know what to look for. You will not really be able to judge conformation until an experienced horseman has pointed each fault out to you, and you will already know what it indicates and what probably caused it. Then you will be able to spot good or bad conformation yourself. But it takes years of observation to be able to judge conformation accurately.

The most important faults to watch for are as follows:

A straight shoulder is one which has little or no slope from the withers to the point of shoulder. This causes a short, choppy stride. It is particularly bad for jumping because a straight-shouldered horse will generally take an extra short step before taking off and will land roughly and stiffly. When you are on a horse with a straight shoulder you will feel as if you are sitting on his neck, for there will be little or nothing in front of you.

A horse who is over in the knees has knees which protrude in front and look slightly bent when viewed from the side, instead of being straight. The forearm will appear slightly further forward than the cannon bone. This is a serious weakness, and will cause a horse to stumble often or to fall when landing after a jump. Many horses

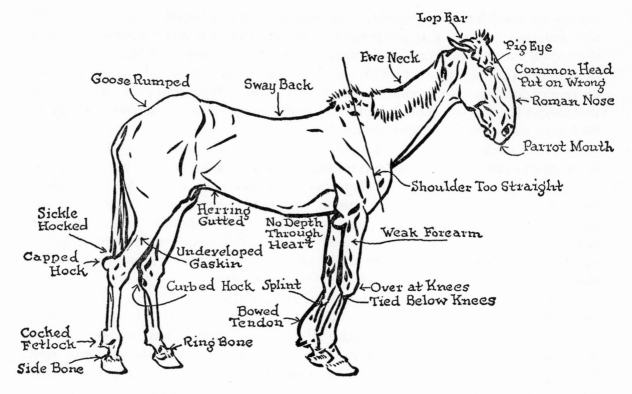

Lop Ear
Pig Eye
Common Head
Put on Wrong
Roman Nose
Parrot Mouth
Shoulder Too Straight
Ewe Neck
Sway Back
Goose Rumped
Herring Gutted
No Depth Through Heart
Weak Forearm
Sickle Hocked
Capped Hock
Undeveloped Gaskin
Curbed Hock Splint
Over at Knees
Tied Below Knees
Bowed Tendon
Cocked Fetlock
Ring Bone
Side Bone

BAD CONFORMATION AND UNSOUNDNESS

are born this way, but it is difficult to recognize it until they are fairly mature, usually two or three years old. More often, though, it is caused by excessive jumping or galloping before the bones have developed sufficiently. Horses should be jumped very little before their third year, and should not jump more than four feet until the end of the third year. The horses that make sensational open jumpers as three-year-olds are seldom heard of after the age of five, when most horses are just beginning.

Two other serious weaknesses of the front leg are the calf knee, which seems to bend backward and causes stiff gaits due to a lack of resilience, and being tied in below the knee, which means that the cannon bone is smaller and weaker at one point.

A long cannon bone is bad for jumping, putting too much strain on the ligaments and tendon, which is apt to bow. Also, a horse with a long cannon bone is seldom a good mover, for he will move higher from the ground than the horse with a short cannon bone. A good mover is called a "grass-cutter" or a "daisy-cutter," meaning that he moves very close to the ground. Such a mover invariably has a good short cannon in front, and a slightly longer one behind.

Long pasterns are a weakness, particularly for jumping, because of the strain they put on the tendons and ligaments. The pastern acts as a shock absorber, for each time a horse's foot hits the ground the shock is absorbed first by the frog and then by the pastern. As the weight of the horse is placed on the leg, the fetlock lowers, and if the pastern is too long, the fetlock will drop too far, nearly hitting the ground, and straining the lower leg. As the weight of the horse is displaced from that foot to another, the fetlock springs up again. A long pastern gives a great deal of spring because it causes the fetlock to drop farther, making the distance back to the normal position that much greater. This results in a lovely, comfortable gait, but so great a strain invites injury, especially in the tremendous impact of landing after a jump.

Too short a pastern, on the other hand, is too static to absorb shock sufficiently, and the concussion travels on up the leg to the knee or shoulder, causing injury. Furthermore, the gaits of a horse with short pasterns are usually quite stiff. The right-size pastern is very important and can generally be judged according to its proportion to the rest of the leg and body. If you cannot judge it by this you will be able to see it when the horse trots, for the long pastern drops too close to the ground, while the short pastern hardly moves at all. A good pastern will show just enough flexibility.

The horse's foot is extremely important and should be in proportion to the rest of his body. It should be broad at the heel and well rounded in front, while the hind foot should be slightly more oval in shape. The inside should show a concave sole which should not be too hard, with adequate room for the frog, which should be large, prominent and elastic. The frog is the horse's shock absorber, preventing the concussion from traveling up through the walls of the foot. The heel should be of medium height, for too low a heel places too much strain on the horse's tendons besides being a source of lameness in itself. This can, however, often be corrected with a high-heeled shoe.

A contracted foot is a serious fault and can sometimes be caused by defective shoeing. In a contracted foot the horny hoof does not allow enough room for the sole and the frog and pinches the foot at the heel. A horse with contracted feet usually develops either ringbone, a bony growth above the foot or on the pastern, or sidebones, the hardening of cartilage just above the coronet band. These both cause serious lameness while they are developing. Ringbone almost always causes permanent lameness, while sidebones, once they are set, do not always impair soundness.

Too long a foot, or a coon foot, puts too much pressure on the heel, with effects similar to those of too low a heel. It also causes a horse to stumble easily. Too large a foot is clumsy and causes a horse to interfere, hitting tendons, fetlocks and heels with his other feet.

The hoof itself should not be too hard or cracked. A toe crack indicates improper shoeing and a brittle hoof. A quarter crack, near the heel, causes painful lameness and is often found in a dry foot or in one which has had too great concussion, such as excessive work on hard roads.

The hind legs should be straight, as viewed from the rear. When seen from the side, the hock, cannon bone and fetlock should be perfectly straight, and a line dropped from the horse's rump to the ground should be slightly behind the point of the hock.

Cow hocks, or hocks which turn in, cause bad movement of the hind feet, which is called winging. They travel in a circular motion rather than straight. Sickle hocks, or hocks which are excessively curved from the bottom of the rump to the point of hock, as viewed from the side, indicate a weak hind leg and lack sufficient strength for jumping. Curbed hocks, or hocks with a lumpiness just below the point of hock, are often the result of sickle hocks, and are common on jumping horses where there has been a great deal of strain. A curb does not seem to affect soundness or strength, but is a conformation fault. Capped hocks are hocks with a lumpiness at the point of hock. This is generally caused by stable kicking and is seldom the cause of lameness.

A bowed tendon can appear on either front or hind legs and is a permanent thickening of the tendon behind the cannon bone. It causes lameness while developing but not after it has set, unless great strain is placed on that leg. It is a serious defect because it is extremely weak. It is generally caused by terrific strain on the tendons, such as a fast start from a standstill or jumping out of heavy, muddy footing.

Splints also occur on either front or back legs and are caused by overwork when a horse is young and his bones have not finished developing. A splint is a bony growth along the cannon bone and does not cause lameness after it has set unless the horse should hit it with another foot, and often will disappear if blistered.

Mutton withers, or thick, muscly withers which conceal the bone, are unattractive and cause the saddle to slide back easily. A mutton-withered horse is also prone to sore withers.

A sway-back, or caved-in back, is very weak and should not be expected to carry too much weight. A hog-back is a high, straight back, usually accompanied by a too-sloping croup, and though strong, it is uncomfortable and causes the saddle to slip forward.

A slab-sided horse is a horse with an extremely narrow rib cage and usually a narrow chest as well. He generally lacks stamina. The chest should be wide with the front legs set squarely. A narrow-chested horse is said to have "both legs coming out of the same hole," causing poor movement in front.

A long-backed horse is one with too much distance between the last rib and the point of hip. This distance should be about the width of an outspread hand. A long back is weak and often means weak kidneys. It is bad for weight carrying, though a long-backed horse is often referred to as a "family horse" because there appears to be room for the entire family on him. He will usually have a long, comfortable stride, however.

A bull neck, or thick, short, muscled neck is unattractive and indicates a tendency to bore on the bit. A ewe neck, or scrawny, rubbery neck, is both unattractive and unpleasant. A ewe-necked horse will have his head in your lap most of the time and is hard to control because he carries his head so high and often puts his tongue over the bit. Martingales seldom help and you usually have to carry your hands high on such a horse. A ewe-necked horse is said to have his neck on upside down.

A wind-broken, or "windy," horse makes a great deal of noise as he breathes *inward*. He often grunts over his fences, which is one of the first signs. To test a horse for windiness you gallop him awhile and then stop, and you will hear a heavy rattling. Heavy breathing as he exhales is natural and should not be mistaken for windiness. It usually occurs in large horses, and is usually caused by serious illness, such as pneumonia, or sudden and excessive overwork. The noise is caused by the growth of a membrane between the two vocal chords and as wind is drawn in, the membrane vibrates. A veterinarian can operate on this by removing the membrane through an incision in the throat, but the operation is not usually entirely successful. A windy horse cannot be worked too heavily or for any extreme length of time, for it is possible for the membrane to break and choke him if he is forced to breathe too heavily.

These are just some of the many unsoundnesses and faults you may find, but they are the major ones which may necessarily affect your choice of a horse. More important, however, they should help you to understand your horse's handicaps and the limit of his capabilities.

SUMMARY

An understanding of a horse's conformation is important so that we will not ask him to do that which he is physically unable to do. Conformation for any breed or type is judged against what has proved to be the best build for its purpose. A horse with good conformation will not necessarily be any better for your individual purposes than one with poor conformation, so your consideration of it should be in accordance with what you want from your horse. Some faults which are considered serious in the show ring may not affect your choice of a horse. The only faults which you must watch out for are those which cause serious weakness or chronic lameness.

CHAPTER IV

The Seat

As LONG AS THE SPORT of riding exists, there will be as many theories of how to sit a horse as there are riders. Every horseman has his own ideas as to which seat is best, based on his own experience, observation and experimentation. His individual seat has been developed to bring him the results he wants. Each horseman has started with one of the established seats — Forward, Military, English, Italian, Spanish School, Park, Balance, Western, or others — and has interpreted it to suit his own needs. But each horseman had to learn the fundamentals before he could develop his own style, just as a pianist must learn scales and technique before he can develop his style. Any rider must learn the principles of the seat.

There are two primary bases for any seat: first, security of the rider, and second, noninterference of the rider with the horse. These are both sound premises as they are both aimed at safety as well as good performances.

The greatest hazard when working with any animal is the uncertainty of his actions. You can never be sure of a horse. He is so much bigger and stronger than you that if he should get out of control or be able to unseat you, you are completely at his mercy. The rider, therefore, must have the most secure seat he possibly can so that he can concentrate fully on keeping his horse under control. Without security in the saddle, you are no rider, only a temporary passenger.

The principle of noninterference may sound contradictory to keeping your horse under control at all times, but it is not. Noninterference only means that the rider must not hamper the horse's natural ability and movements. Your weight on his back interferes with his way of going, so it should be kept to a minimum by correct placement. For example, a horse may be perfectly able to jump a four-foot fence, but if the rider's weight should land on his back in the middle of the fence it would cause him to hit it with his hind legs. Or if the rider had to yank on the reins in the middle of the jump in order to maintain his own balance, it would interfere with the horse's balance, causing him to jump badly or even to hit the fence hard enough in front

18

to turn him over. So besides ruining the performance, interference increases the danger of accidents.

The two major points of a seat which will increase the rider's security and lessen his interference with the horse are flexibility and equilibrium. These are of equal importance and the essence of a good, safe seat on a horse. They must be concentrated on from your first moment in the saddle.

Flexibility is resilience, or elasticity of your body, and in order for your body to be flexible, it must be *completely* relaxed. You cannot succeed in any sport with tense muscles. The key to sports is co-ordination, not strength, and the fundamental principle of co-ordination is *relaxation*. That is why, when you watch top sportsmen in any field, the sport always looks so easy — a swimmer glides so effortlessly through the water, a tennis player's stroke is so graceful. Power in sport is not through strength but skill.

Flexibility is not, of course, a positive action, but a passive reaction to the movements of your horse. It is not something you can consciously *do*, but something which you unconsciously *are*. If your body is flexible, you are adaptable and responsive to your horse's actions. Resilience is absorbing the movements of your horse, which is what makes the rider look smooth. A horse moves very quickly, and in that split second between the horse's movement and your positive reaction to it, your body must respond sympathetically. That is, your body must not resist the movement, which would throw you off balance, but should move with it. For instance, if your horse should suddenly shy and your body were stiff and resistant, you would find yourself sitting on air. But if your body were flexible, you would move *with* your horse, and still be well-balanced and able to bring him back immediately and convince him that there was nothing there to frighten him. It's a matter of being *with* your horse rather than perched *on top* of him.

Equilibrium is only balance, but balance is a big word. It is not easy to retain your balance at all times when you are on an active animal. You cannot keep your balance unless you are flexible in the saddle, for if you are stiff, you will lose it with every sudden movement. Equilibrium is the first thing that worries you when you start to ride — you're afraid of falling off, which is simply losing your balance. You grab the reins for balance, and this hurts the horse's mouth and makes him stop short, and you fall off. Then you try holding on to the pommel of the saddle, but this doesn't work because it pinches your fingers and prevents you from holding the reins at all. The only aid you have until you have learned to keep your balance is the horse's mane. You can hold on to that without hurting your horse, and you can still hold the reins. During my first years of riding it was balance and the mane that kept me aboard, because my legs were too short to give me any security — they only reached halfway down the skirt of the saddle. I have pictures of myself over four-foot fences

19

where I was at least a foot above my horse, with no contact other than my hands clutching the mane. Somehow when he landed I landed on his back again, regained my balance, and rode for the next fence.

On the basis of these four factors — security, noninterference, flexibility and equilibrium — we have chosen a modified and serviceable seat, which we will not classify and limit with any name at all. It is more forward than the English seat, less stiff than the American military seat, and less extreme than the true forward seat. It is a natural seat, for both the rider and the horse. It is comfortable, secure and powerful. It is the easiest seat for a beginner to learn, yet it is an excellent foundation for any interpretation the accomplished rider may wish to give it. It is a basic seat. And remember, it's easier to learn to ride the right way than the wrong way. The latter may seem quicker, but it doesn't go as far!

Whatever seat you are going to ride, you have to evaluate your own conformation, to see just how *you* are put together. Your body is your basic tool in riding, so your anatomy is going to have a bearing on how quickly you will be able to learn to ride, what kind of horse will suit you best, and on what part of your body you will have to concentrate the greatest effort.

Riding is a very active sport — more active than most. It is akin to tennis, swimming or skiing in its demands upon the body. It utilizes almost every muscle in your body — you know this after your first ride, when you seem to ache all over! The combination of muscles used in riding is different from the combination used in any other sport, and the amount of co-ordination necessary to make these muscles work in unison is tremendous. Co-ordination is probably the most difficult part of riding. Most people who have been active in other sports have fairly good co-ordination, but they still have to learn to co-ordinate different muscles, different parts of the body. People who have little or no co-ordination will have to spend that many more hours in the saddle until they have learned it. They will have trouble, for example, in using one leg and not the other, or even in using their legs without moving their hands at the same time.

Co-ordination is what will help you overcome physical "handicaps" in riding. You may have long legs, for instance, which will be difficult to control on a horse, but by concentrating on them, you will eventually be able to keep them still with good co-ordination.

Our bodies are not only the result of how we were born, but of what has been done with them — training, exercise or sports — throughout our lives. Some of these things are advantages, some handicaps. Some people have strong hands, for example, and some have sensitive hands, but for riding your hands must be neither too strong, nor too sensitive, but a little of each. As soon as we can evaluate our handicaps, they cease to be handicaps and we can compensate for them with our good points.

20

HORSEMANSHIP

The perfect body for riding, however, is fairly common, especially among young-sters. It is lean, well-proportioned, sinewy and supple. This is such an advantage that anyone with such a body is called a "natural" because he can sit very naturally on a horse, is comfortable on any size or shape of horse, and usually has rather good coordination.

The second most wonderful attribute you can have for riding is natural rhythm, or feeling. This is similar to co-ordination, but it is something which you can't just *learn* — it has to *happen*. It's something you either have or you haven't, and if you haven't got it, you'll spend hours in the saddle until it comes to you. After I had been riding a couple of years I reached the point where I simply had to have more feeling in order to ride well. My instructor knew from my riding that I lacked all sense of rhythm. He bet me that I couldn't dance — I couldn't! So, though I thought him insane at that point, I followed his advice and went through a siege of dancing lessons (which I detested) and incredibly enough, it did improve my riding. I learned to feel every muscle in my horse's body. I knew what he was going to do before *he* knew it!

For horsemanship, the body is divided into three basic parts: the upper body, which is the portion between the head and the hips; the seat, which consists of the hips through the knees, or the part of the body which actually contacts the saddle; and the lower leg, which is the leg from the knee to the toe. These are the three parts which must be co-ordinated to make the whole. If one of these parts is out of position, it will throw the other two parts out also.

Certain rules govern the position of each part of the body in order to make a safe, secure seat possible. They are as follows:

The basis of your seat and security on a horse is your foot, for if this is not correct, the rest of the leg cannot be correct. The weight of your entire body is centered over your feet, and this weight will push your heels down. The stirrup should support the foot at the most comfortable point, which is generally the ball of the foot, nearer the instep than the toe. This position of the stirrup makes it easier to put your weight in your heels and to avoid relying upon the stirrups for the actual support of the whole body. If you ride with your stirrups "home," or at the instep of your foot, your whole leg will be much stiffer and it will be harder to keep your weight in your heels. You must never push on your stirrups or depend upon them for your security; your security is in your legs. With your weight in your heels so that they are well down you will not lose your stirrups, so if your feet *do* slip out of the stirrups it means that your weight is not in your heels.

Your toes should turn outwards ever so slightly, at no more than a fifteen or twenty degree angle. If you turn your toes out at a greater angle your whole leg will turn out, for it is impossible to keep your leg straight and against your horse with your feet in such an exaggerated position. Do not try to wrap your legs around your

21

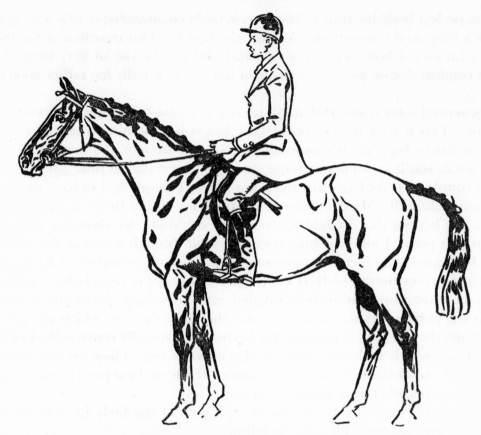

POSITION AT THE STANDSTILL
Note the straight line from the horse's mouth to the rider's elbow.

horse by clinging with your heels against his sides either, for this completely ruins the rest of the leg and your grip is lost.

Your ankle is comparable to the horse's fetlock in that it is your shock absorber. When you walk or run, your weight and the concussion of your foot's impact against the ground are absorbed naturally by your ankle. On a horse, as you post at a trot, for example, the weight in your heels will naturally increase as you rise from your saddle. As you sit again the weight decreases. Since neither the stirrup nor the heel can rise up and down as this weight increases and decreases something has to give, and that give is in your ankle, as well as in your knees. For their work as shock absorbers your ankles must be completely relaxed and flexible, and this is best achieved with the ankle in a "broken" position. This means that your ankle must bend inward, toward your horse. If your weight is in your heels, this will not be difficult, though it may take time for you to get it just right. If your ankle is relaxed and "broken," it will be very comfortable, and your leg will not stiffen and tire after long hours of riding. A "broken" ankle will give you good balance and flexibility. A stiff ankle will make your whole body stiff and your movements jerky.

If your ankles and feet are in the correct position, your calves will rest naturally against the horse's sides, for the insides, not the backs, of the calves are an important part of your grip. The lower part of the calf should be close to your horse's side so that you need only apply pressure for an increase of speed or other leg aids. The ankle and heel, however, should be out away from the horse's side, otherwise they will be a source of constant irritation to the horse, as well as turning your knee out. For greater strength in the leg aids you may kick your horse *from this position* of the heel, bringing it against the horse's side immediately behind the girth. Never bring your leg further back to kick him, and never move your leg further away from his side in order to kick him. These two methods greatly lessen your security and throw you off balance. If your horse is insensitive to an ordinary short kick, use a crop — don't ruin your position. A straight line dropped down from your knee should just hit the tip of your toe. You should never be able to see your toe in front of your knee as you look down at it.

A common mistake in riding is to try to get security by squeezing your knees against the saddle. Your security is in your whole leg, particularly your lower thigh, the *inside* of your knee, and the inside of your calf. If your foot and calf are in the correct position, it will be very difficult to pinch with your knee, for this would throw your lower calf and foot way out from your horse and make it impossible to keep your weight in your heels. Furthermore, extreme pressure of the knees indicates to your horse that you want an increase of speed, especially on a well-schooled horse. There should never, however, be any daylight between your knees and the saddle. The best exercises for learning the proper grip of the legs is riding bareback, which makes you use your lower leg for grip and not your knees alone, and riding without stirrups, which prevents you from depending on your stirrups for support.

Your seat should rest naturally in the saddle, with the crotch close to the pommel and the distance of the width of a hand between your seat and the cantle of the saddle. The actual position of the seat will be determined by the position of the upper body, but the important thing is to have a "deep" seat; sink down into the saddle.

The posture of the upper body is actually determined by the position of the lower leg and by the length of the stirrups. The upper body should be erect, at a right angle to the horse's back at a standstill or walk, and inclined *slightly* further forward at increased gaits. The position at the canter varies slightly from this, as you will see in the next chapter. The shoulders should be thrown back, head high, chest out, and there should be a very slight hollow in your back at the waist. Your head must *always* be held up by keeping your *eyes up* at all times. Look through his ears or higher, and always watch where you are going. Never look down at your horse, or at the ground, or you'll find yourself sitting on it! Furthermore, if your head is down you will not only see nothing, but you will ruin the position of the rest of your body, rounding your back. When the back is rounded, or the shoulders hunched, it is appropriately called a "roach back." It is unattractive and ineffective.

Your arms should hang naturally from your shoulders, with your elbows close to your sides, in a comfortable position. Never thrust your elbows outward — you'll look like Ichabod Crane! Your lower arms, hands and reins should form a straight line from the horse's mouth to your elbow. Your hands should be held a few inches above and in front of the horse's withers, about forty-five degrees off the horizontal. That is, your thumbs should be slightly higher than the outer edges of your hands, but never sticking straight up. This oblique position is the most natural and is best for the application of the rein aids.

The one element which draws all these individual parts into a harmonious whole is *equilibrium*. You can't ignore equilibrium when you are off a horse without falling down, and it's just as important *on* a horse. Picture an imaginary line drawn from the top of your head to the ground. At a standstill and a walk this line is perpendicular to the ground. At the trot or gallop, the top of this line of equilibrium is further forward because of inertia. Just as when you are standing on a bus you must lean forward to maintain your balance because of the inertia of the moving vehicle, you must lean slightly forward on a horse at an increased gait when you are out of the saddle. It's a matter of gravity. When you are sitting at a canter, however, it's like sitting on a moving vehicle — there is no need to lean forward. But at the gallop you have two-point contact, which means you are out of the saddle, so it is necessary to lean well forward to keep your balance.

The length of your stirrups is also important in the position of your body and the maintenance of equilibrium. If your stirrups are too short, you will have less security. The knee angle will close, making it more acute. This means that in order to keep your balance you will have to close the body angle (at the hip) by leaning further forward. If the stirrups are too long, the knee angle will be opened, so to keep your balance you will have to open the body angle by leaning backward. The correct length of stirrup is between the two, and is best measured by hanging your leg out of the stirrup and alongside it, and adjusting the stirrup strap until the bottom of the stirrup hits your leg just below your inside ankle bone.

The only way you will be able to understand these basic rules of position thoroughly is to try them on a horse. Put them to the test — you'll find them worthy.

HORSEMANSHIP

SUMMARY

Regardless of what seat you are riding, there are certain principles which you must understand before you can know what you are trying to accomplish. The basic aims are security of the rider and noninterference of the rider with the horse. The ways to achieve these are flexibility and relaxation of the rider and perfect equilibrium or balance, and these are brought together through co-ordination and rhythm, both of which are achieved only by complete relaxation of the rider. The principles of position are summarized by an old saying: "Your head and your heart hold high, your heels and your hands hold low."

CHAPTER V

Position at the Increased Gaits

YOUR POSITION in the saddle at the various gaits is, primarily, the basis upon which your riding is judged. A certain degree of perfection is required at these gaits before you are asked to prove your actual riding ability in the use of the aids and the mastery of your horse.

When you have really learned the principles of the position at the standstill and walk, you are ready to concentrate on your position at the increased gaits — trot, canter and gallop. If you have started out with the correct position it should not take very long to have a good position at the increased gaits. If you have ridden much without paying attention to position, it will take quite a while to correct your mistakes. At the increased gaits each element of the seat as described in the last chapter is more important and harder to do because everything happens faster and you also have to think about controlling your horse. You *must* keep your heels down, your eyes up, your legs in the correct position and every part of your body in the right place.

Position is most important for security and also for appearance. When your position is automatic you are able to concentrate on the more important points — application of the aids and the actual mastery of your horse. With a good position, a rider who is poor in ability and experience can look very smooth and better than he is. Eventually his knowledge and ability will catch up with his appearance and he will be a good rider.

The correct position at the increased gaits also prepares you for jumping long before you see a fence. It is comparatively easy to learn to jump when you already have security, balance and flexibility, and know how to ride without interfering with your horse.

Sometimes as your actual riding ability increases it is almost more difficult than ever to retain a good position. You may, for example, be concentrating fully on the use of your legs. As you work harder on your legs they may slip further and further behind the girth, and your upper body will incline further forward in order to keep your balance. You will look like a "monkey on a stick" and will have to lengthen your stirrups for a while and concentrate on getting your legs back to normal. Then you might go to the other extreme and get your legs too far forward, either throwing your upper body forward, like a jackknife, to counteract your legs, or you might lose your balance completely and lean too far back with your upper body. Whenever your upper body is out of position, you know there is something wrong with some other part of your body. This can happen to any rider.

POSITION AT THE TROT
The rider is balanced over his legs.

The inclination of the upper body at the trot is mainly determined by equilibrium, but the exact amount of inclination is actually dependent upon the gait and thrust of your horse. Do not get ahead of your horse by leaning so far forward that your own weight is ahead of your base of support.

The most important point in trotting is to let your horse do the work for you. Do not try to post until the thrust of his gait throws you out of the saddle. The movement of the horse's hind leg at the trot is what will thrust you upward and forward. Do not move any further out of the saddle than necessary, because you want to post as smoothly and inconspicuously as possible. A horse with a short stride will give you very little thrust, and such a horse is very good for horsemanship because he will make you look very smooth and your posting will look completely effortless. A horse with a long stride will throw you much higher from the saddle, but there is no horse with so long a stride as to thrust you far enough to cause your legs to straighten out, though it is often seen. The inexperienced rider invariably feels compelled to rise as far out of the saddle as possible, as though he were actually standing up and sitting down. The rider should look as if he were barely moving at all.

In the first place, when you have given your horse the command to trot, you must simply *sit* until he actually breaks from the slow trot to the full trot. When he does break, the movement of his hind legs will force you to post, throwing you upward and forward. Sit, wait, and when you can no longer sit, then you post. Always wait for your horse!

Since it is the work of the hind leg to thrust you out of your saddle, the burden is obviously greater for one hind leg than it is for the other. This is why diagonals are very important. When working on a straight line, or on the bridle path, you should change diagonals intermittently in order to equalize the burden and, therefore, the development of the horse's hind legs. When working in the ring or in circles, diagonals are even more important. Moving in a circle, the horse's outside hind leg has the greater distance to travel, and the inside leg the shorter distance. It is necessary then that the leg with the shorter distance to travel be given the added burden of thrusting the rider out of the saddle. When moving to the right, the right hind leg has the shorter distance to cover; when moving to the left, the left hind leg has the shorter distance. Trotting is a diagonal gait: the right hind and left front legs move at approximately the same moment, and the left hind and right front legs move together. So, if the *inside* hind leg throws you up, you will come down again on the opposite front leg, i.e., the *outside* front leg, as it hits the ground. If the right hind leg thrusts you up, you will land in the saddle again as the left front lands on the ground. So, if you are working in a circle to the right, you should come down with the left front leg, which means that you are on the left diagonal. If you are working in a circle to the left, you must come down with the right front leg, which means that you are on the right diagonal. In this way the inside leg will always be the one to thrust you out of your saddle.

Now it's not necessary to lean over and look under your horse to see which foot is where in order to know if you're on the correct diagonal or not. Simply watch your horse's shoulder. If you are in the saddle as the right shoulder moves toward you, you are on the right diagonal; if the right shoulder moves away from you as you are in the saddle, you are on the left diagonal. In other words, the outside shoulder (the one nearest the rail) should always move toward you as you are sitting and away from you as you rise. Moving in a circle toward the right, the left shoulder should be back as you sit; moving in a circle toward the left, the right shoulder should be back as you sit. After you have been riding awhile, you will not even have to look at your horse's shoulder — you will be able to feel which diagonal is correct because the correct one is so much smoother than the wrong one. Since the stride of the outside hind leg is longer than that of the inside, it will throw you further out of the saddle and cause you to post higher. When you are on the correct diagonal it is the *inside* hind leg which thrusts you out of the saddle, not the outside hind leg. It's a good idea to work in small figure eights at a trot until you can feel the difference between the correct and wrong diagonal.

Because diagonals have such an effect on your horse and on your own smoothness, they are very important in the show ring, and they also show you know a little something about what you are doing.

There are two different ways to post — with the motion of your horse, or behind the motion. Posting with the motion means that you are working *with* your horse's stride, being as little hindrance to him as possible because you are keeping most of your weight off his back. What weight there is is centered over his forehand. Posting behind the motion means that you are with his stride but counteracting it with the placement of your weight on his back. This is only good when done for a purpose, such as slowing down a bold horse or schooling a green horse.

Learning to post with the motion is very important because it is more comfortable, secure and effective for you and much better for your horse. In posting with the motion the movement of your seat is almost circular. Your horse throws you upward and forward and then instead of falling back and down again, you simply sink straight down on your *crotch,* not your seat, and the movement of your horse will then make you slide back into position again. Do not lean any further forward, for this would get you ahead of your horse, ruining your balance and security. Posting with the motion is often difficult to learn, but the results are so wonderful that it will be well worth it.

Posting behind the motion is not posting behind the stride of your horse, as so many beginners do. You must still have the correct position in order to do it, but the movement of the seat is different from that of posting with the motion. After you have been thrust upward and forward you simply come back and down again, landing on the buttocks instead of the crotch. The placement of your weight is further back and thus hinders your horse in his stride and pace. That is why it is good on a bold or a green horse. It is not actually as comfortable or flexible as posting with the motion, nor does it look as smooth.

Posting with the motion is the best preparation for jumping known because of the action of the hip angle. When you post with the motion, your hip angle remains nearly closed, while the knee angles open and close as you rise and sit. In jumping, the hip angle must also remain as nearly closed as possible so that the rider will not get too far out of the saddle and too far forward, completely destroying his security in the saddle. The action of the rider in posting with the motion is ideally the action of the rider over a fence.

POSITION AT THE CANTER — THREE-POINT CONTACT
This is not the sitting canter. The position at the sitting canter is exactly the same as at the standstill.

The position of the rider at the canter is very different from the trot. In a true hunting seat, in preparation for jumping, you are again down in the saddle, almost as at the walk, but your weight should be on your crotch, as it is in posting with the motion, and the rest of the seat slightly out of the saddle to allow for the action of the horse's hind legs. This is called three-point contact — the crotch and both knees. Your position will depend a great deal upon your horse's gait. If he has a smooth canter you can sit close to the saddle, but with a rough canter you will have to get slightly further out of the saddle, but still maintaining the three-point contact.

HORSEMANSHIP

You should, however, also be able to sit well down in the saddle, as one must in a saddle-horse seat or a park seat. This is the way you should sit in a flat horsemanship class or in a hack class, where you are trying to keep your horse at a slow canter, for rising out of the saddle at all and leaning forward encourages your horse to a faster pace. In order to sit to a canter, the upper body must be absolutely straight, as at a standstill, and you must sit completely in the saddle, regardless of the gait of the horse. This is where relaxation is particularly important, for if your back is tense at any one point you will bounce out of the saddle at every stride. Your body must break at the *hips,* not the waist, and your entire lower body must roll back and forth with the movement of the horse. Your shoulders must remain still, but from your hips down you must give and take with the stride of the horse. This is easiest, of course, with a horse with a very smooth canter, but when you have perfected it you will be able to sit perfectly still on a horse with the roughest canter. You should be so still in the saddle that you could carry a glass full of water without spilling it. If you break at the waist, your whole back will bend and straighten with each stride, as it will if the muscles in the small of your back are tense. Exaggerate it at first, letting

POSITION AT THE GALLOP — TWO-POINT CONTACT
The rider's weight is in her heels entirely.

31

your whole upper body relax completely and be perfectly loose, and after a while you will feel the rhythm of the horse's stride and roll with it. It may take a great deal of practicing, but it is well worth it.

At the hand gallop and gallop, the rider has two-point contact — the knees alone. Because of the action of the horse's hind legs it is necessary to get well out of the saddle, which also encourages the faster pace, because the rider's weight is entirely in his heels, and not on the horse's back. This is the position which you will eventually use in the approach to the fence, though when you are learning to jump, it is best to approach with a three-point contact and a slower pace. At a walk the average horse moves at four miles an hour, at the sitting trot, six miles an hour, and at the trot, eight miles an hour. A horse can jump a small fence at any of these speeds. The speed of the canter is from eight to ten miles an hour; the hand gallop, twelve to fourteen miles an hour; the gallop, sixteen to eighteen miles an hour. Few horses can jump well at a pace exceeding fourteen miles an hour, and most jump best at about twelve miles an hour.

SUMMARY

You are ready to learn the position at the increased gaits only after you have thoroughly learned the position at the standstill and walk and the principles of the seat. You must not exaggerate your position at the increased gaits for it is basically the same as that which you learned at the slower gaits. There are two ways to post — with the motion and behind the motion — and these are a matter of timing more than position. There are two ways to canter — three-point contact and sitting down in the saddle — and of these you may take your choice, but should be able to do both. The position at the hand gallop and gallop is based on two-point contact, and this simulates the actual jumping position.

CHAPTER VI

The Aids

THIS MASTERY of the horse we have been talking about is achieved by one method — the application of the aids. The aids are your controls — like the steering wheel, accelerator and brakes on a car. They are the first thing you must learn, yet something which you will go on learning indefinitely. The correct application of the aids is the skill which is our strength on a horse. It is the essence of fine equitation yet essential from your first moment on a horse. The finesse with which you are able to apply the aids, your ability to conceal their application, will be the measure of your skill. A horse obeying the unseen commands of his rider is indeed a pleasant sight, and a rare one, but this is your aim. With the proper use of the aids you can school your horse to perfection, while the improper application will result in souring him.

There are two kinds of aids: the natural aids — your legs, hands, voice and weight; and the artificial aids — spurs, whips, bits and martingales. The natural aids must be learned first, for they are essentially your horsemanship. You must be able to control your hands and legs and to assist them with your weight and voice. The artificial aids are used to increase the effects of the natural aids.

The most important point in the application of the aids is co-ordination. You must be able to apply two aids at virtually the same time, and yet you must also be able to apply one aid at a time without counteracting it with another. You must not ask your horse to move forward with your legs, for example, while holding him back with your hands. This is called clashing your controls; it's like using the accelerator and the brake on a car at the same time.

Before you can achieve this co-ordination, however, you will have to be secure in your saddle. Your hands and legs must be independent of your body and of one another. Your hands and legs are either active or passive at all times, and unless you are applying one of the aids, they should be passive. But passive hands and legs are steady, relaxed hands and legs, and if yours are not yet steady, you had better work on your position until they are, otherwise you will not have much success in applying the aids. Steady hands are particularly important because the slightest movement of your hands affects your horse's mouth. Eventually you may acquire "educated" hands — hands which automatically apply no more pressure on the horse's mouth than he requires, feeling every give and take of his head.

The legs as an aid are used primarily to increase speed. Pressure of both legs at once is a command to move forward. Don't kick unless you absolutely must; just touch your heel to your horse's side and squeeze with your lower leg. Strong kicking looks dreadful, has little effect, and throws the rider off balance. The amount of pressure to be exerted by your legs depends on both the sensitivity of your horse and the amount of increase which you desire. You should apply this pressure gently at first and increase it as necessary until it has had the effect you wanted. If your horse does not respond, check your hands to be sure you are not holding him back at the same time. If he still does not respond it indicates that a crop is in order, or for the competent rider, the use of spurs. But generally it is the fault of the rider when the horse does not respond. Remember, for forward motion, be sure to relax the reins at the same time you exert pressure with your legs.

The use of one leg at a time is a signal to your horse to move his body to the side. If he has swung his haunches out to the right side, for instance, you should use a strong right leg to bring them back into place. Or if you are making a turn or a circle you should apply pressure with your inside leg, the leg on the inside of the turn or circle, to make his body, as well as his legs, follow the turn.

When you apply pressure with both legs and even greater pressure with your hands, it is a command to the horse to move backwards.

Above all, please do not apply constant pressure with your legs in an effort to gain security. Neither your calves nor your knees should *squeeze* except in applying your leg aids. Constant pressure will only irritate a horse, especially a high-strung one, and eventually his sides will simply become soured to the use of the legs.

The hands and reins together make up the rein aids. There are several kinds of aids, each with a special purpose: direct, indirect, leading, bearing and pulley. The first rein you ever learn to use is the direct rein. This is the rein which you use for decrease of speed and to indicate direction. It is the one rein that forms a perfectly straight line between your horse's mouth and your elbow, and if you do not have a straight line, the effect of the rein is lessened.

To apply the direct rein, you first establish contact with the horse's mouth. That is, you shorten your reins until there is no slack in them, yet no pressure. Then, to apply this aid you simply exert pressure on the reins, and therefore on the horse's mouth, by *closing your hands*. There is no need to pull or yank on his mouth — simply tighten the last two fingers of each hand. The amount of pressure to be applied depends somewhat on the sensitivity of the horse's mouth, the severity of the bit being

THE DIRECT REIN ON THE RIGHT SIDE
Note the straight line between the horse's mouth and the rider's elbow.

used, and the amount of decrease of speed you want. But the strength of this rein lies not in the amount of pressure, but in the steadiness with which the pressure is applied. You must be thoroughly consistent. If you want to slow down from a trot to a walk, for instance, you apply this pressure evenly with both hands *until* he walks, *then* relax the reins. You must not apply it, let go, and apply it again. Once you have made up your mind, *hold* the pressure until he reaches the gait you want, and then release it. This consistency of application is most important with all aids. When you *do* relax the pressure, this is his reward for having obeyed your command. If your horse is not already well schooled he will learn to associate this reward with his obedience and will respond more and more quickly to your commands as time goes on, *if you are consistent.*

If you want to indicate change of direction with the direct rein, you apply more pressure on one rein than you already have on the other. For a turn to the left, for example, you apply pressure to the left rein, in the same manner as explained above, *keeping your hands still and together.*

The leading rein is the rein used occasionally for extreme changes of direction, such as a ninety-degree or greater turn. To apply it you move your hand away from the withers in the direction of the turn and apply pressure. For a turn to the left, you move your left hand away from the withers, apply pressure on that rein, and relax the pressure of your right hand, clearly indicating the direction you want your horse

THE LEADING REIN ON THE LEFT SIDE
The rider's hand may be held farther away from the horse if necessary.

THE BEARING REIN

to follow. You must use your legs at the same time, lest your horse move only his head and not his body.

The bearing rein is very seldom used, except on western horses and polo ponies. They have been schooled to it and respond very quickly. For this rein you take both reins in one hand and move that hand in the direction of movement, applying pressure at the same time. Most of the pressure is applied against the horse's neck on the side opposite the turn, so it is often called a "neck-rein." On horses who are schooled to it, this rein results in a very quick turn, throwing the horse's weight back to his hindquarters and turning his forehand abruptly in the direction of the turn causing him to pivot on his hind legs. In ordinary turns the horse's hindquarters follow his forehand.

THE PULLEY REIN
The rider's left hand is set against the horse's neck. The rider's right hand is applying pressure on the horse's mouth. Both hands may cross the withers if necessary for added pressure on the mouth.

The pulley rein is a very effective and not too well known rein which is used for an immediate halt or decrease of speed. This rein demands a sudden stop by throwing all the horse's weight onto his hindquarters, and it is an excellent way to stop a horse which is out of control. It is applied as follows: the rider applies pressure on both reins and sets one hand on the horse's neck in front of the withers so that hand will be able to hold its pressure no matter how the horse pulls. With the other hand, the rider actually pulls against the horse's mouth, crossing the rein slightly over his withers, so that the horse's neck serves as a fulcrum. Often it is not necessary to cross the rein at all, and a straight direct rein on that side may be used. The pulley rein, applied correctly, will stop any horse on a dime, and give you nine cents change! It is particularly useful in the show ring if you are asked to gallop and stop at a certain point. It can be used very smoothly, too, if you keep your hands fairly close together and do not actually pull on the rein which is not set. With this severe rein aid it is particularly important that you relax the pressure the moment your horse has obeyed, for if you continue the pressure your horse will probably start to back up or even rear. It's a very strong rein and should only be used when really necessary.

The indirect reins of opposition are the most complicated rein aids, though not at all difficult to apply. The indirect reins serve to displace the horse's weight from one foot to another or from the forehand to the hindquarters, which is necessary for many movements, including the departure into the canter. They are the reins which control not only his front or hindquarters, but his entire body. There are two kinds of indirect reins — in front of the withers and behind the withers.

THE RIGHT INDIRECT REIN IN FRONT OF THE WITHERS—AS SEEN FROM THE SIDE

The indirect rein of opposition in front of the withers transfers the horse's weight from one forefoot to the other, freeing one for action. This is the indirect rein most often used, and with outstanding results. It is used in everyday riding. To apply this aid, you establish contact with both reins, then moving one hand just over the front of the horse's withers, you apply pressure on that rein. If you want to place his weight on his left foot, you use the right indirect rein; for the right foot, you use the left indirect rein. This rein will bring the horse's nose out slightly to the side on which you have applied the rein. When making a circle or a turn, you use the inside rein, or the rein on the inside of the circle or turn. This places his weight on his outside forefoot, and with the use of the rider's inside leg will make the horse's body follow the turn instead of remaining stiff and straight. With a well-schooled horse it is not necessary actually to cross the horse's withers with your hand, so this rein can be applied very inconspicuously. This is also the rein used for the turn on the fore-hand, planting one foot as a pivot and leaving the other free to move.

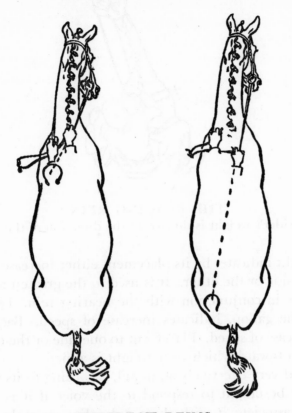

INDIRECT REINS

1. The indirect rein in front of the withers places the horse's weight on the opposite front foot. Here the right rein places the weight on the left front foot.
2. The indirect rein behind the withers places the horse's weight on the opposite hind foot. Here the right rein places the weight on the left hind foot.

The indirect rein of opposition behind the withers serves to transfer the horse's weight from one hind foot to the other and from front to hind. This rein is applied in the same manner as the indirect rein in front of the withers except that the rider's hand crosses just behind the withers. The length of your rein does not usually allow you actually to cross the horse's withers, but you move your hand as far as necessary in that direction. The right indirect rein behind the withers places the horse's weight on his left hind foot, the left indirect rein behind the withers places the weight on the right hind foot. This rein is used in the turn on the haunches, freeing his forehand to make the turn and planting his hind leg as a pivot.

THE BEARING REIN
The rider's weight is thrown in the direction of the turn.

The rider's weight indicates by its placement either increase or decrease of speed, or movement to one side or the other. It is used to the greatest advantage on western horses or polo ponies in conjunction with the bearing rein. Forward placement of weight, such as at the gallop, indicates increase of speed. Backward placement of weight indicates decrease of speed. Placement to one side or the other indicates movement in the direction toward which your weight is aimed.

The voice is used very effectively as an aid, according to its volume and tone. A horse can very easily be taught to respond to the voice if it is used with the other aids so that he will associate it with those aids. For example, if you sternly call, "Whoa," each time you bring your horse to a halt, he will eventually come to a halt with the use of the voice alone. If you ask for a walk, trot or canter each time you put him into those gaits he may learn to associate the sound and intonation of the words with the gait you want. Many horses who have done a great deal of ring work have learned to obey the voice commands of the ringmaster. The horse who will respond to the voice command to decrease speed or halt is particularly delightful in the show ring, where you want the best obedience, but better still, his mouth is saved and he will have greater respect for the reins when they are used.

Now for the artificial aids — spurs, bits, whips and martingales — which will amplify the effects of the natural aids. Actually, artificial aids are those implements made by man to help him where he lacks skill or patience in conquering the horse, and they are, therefore, available in varying degrees of severity. I do not mean that all artificial aids are barbaric — of course they are not. Obviously one cannot ride a horse which has no bit in his mouth. But too often the lazy or unskilled rider has

HORSEMANSHIP

recourse to the most brutal bits or spurs, using them incorrectly at that. And there are the angry riders who, having failed through their own incompetence, take most unfair advantage of their whips. This is not only poor sportsmanship, but sheer stupidity. Much more would be achieved by the rider's correcting his own mistakes than by punishing his horse for them.

Every piece of equipment devised to help us with horses has its place, but all of them are too often misused. These are spurs, whips and bits which should never be used for anything but an occasional schooling, for most horses schooled with such severe weapons are not likely to forget such a schooling in a hurry. Even martingales are often used incredibly badly and dangerously, strapping a horse's head down so that he can't even use it when he needs it, especially in jumping. Malpractice with the artificial aids is so widespread among would-be horsemen that it is appalling and frightening.

In the first place, those riders who, lacking skill, find it necessary to resort to the more severe types of equipment are precisely the ones in whose hands these aids are most dangerous. The more severe the bit or spur, the more skillfully it should be applied, in order to achieve the desired effects. All too often have we seen horses with gashed and bloody sides due to the constant scraping of roweled spurs on uncontrolled legs; or horses driven nearly insane for lack of breath due to a hackamore bit in the erratic hands of an unbalanced rider. Granted, some horses have mouths so calloused that a hackamore, which exerts pressure on the nostrils rather than the mouth, is necessary, but only in the hands of a skilled rider is this a reasonable bit. Even roweled spurs are sometimes necessary on a soured horse, but these should only be on the steadiest legs. Most horses don't need such severe treatment, and if a rider can't use a decent bit on a horse he should get off him and ride for another hundred hours until he's ready for such a horse.

Probably the first artificial aid which you will be called upon to use is the crop, or whip. You will need this on horses who will not respond to your leg pressure when you want an increase of speed. Occasionally you will need it as punishment, but only in particular circumstances, such as a refusal at a fence. There are several kinds of whips and these may be used even by the inexperienced rider once he has been taught how to apply this aid. It is far better to resort to a crop when a horse does not respond to your legs than to squirm about in the saddle, kicking furiously.

The whip should be held in one hand, the handle upwards and the length of the whip resting along the horse's shoulder. When you want to use the whip, take both reins in your free hand, let go of the reins with your whip hand, and quickly reach back behind the saddle and hit your horse's side between his ribs and his hip. The purpose is not to beat the horse, but to startle him by the noise and sting of the whip, so the stroke should be quick and decisive, but not brutal. On the other hand, if you're

41

going to use the whip, use it so that your horse feels it. A weak tap will more likely amuse than chastise him and will be a waste of time and effort.

The best and most commonly used whip is the feathered bat, which is generally the one used in the show ring. This is made of whalebone for flexibility, and is covered with braided leather halfway down. The bottom half is covered with fringed, or feathered, leather so that it will sting your horse and make enough noise to frighten him. There is also a leather tab on the end.

Novices often use a plain straight whip which, in an exaggerated length, is used by saddle-horse riders. This is generally made of whalebone and is longer than the feathered bat. It is covered with braided leather and tapers toward the end, which usually has some sort of tab on it. These crops often have a loop for the hand at the top, but it is best either to remove the loop or disregard it, for any equipment which dangles from the rider and yet is attached to him in some way offers a hazard and could cause an accident.

In the hunting field, of course, the hunting crop is used. This is a stiff, heavy whip with a right-angled handle of bone and a hard shank of about one and a half or two feet in length. Attached to the shank is a heavy, tapering, braided leather thong with a thread lash at the end, in the color of your hunt. These are cumbersome to carry because of the length of the thong, but they are extremely helpful in the hunting field. The handle is easily used by the rider in reaching down from his horse to open and close gates, and, of course, the crop's prime purpose is to whip-in hounds by snapping it. Few people other than the officers of the hunt have occasion to use it for this, but you may at some point be extremely helpful by being able to round up a stray hound with it. This whip is also carried in horse-show classes which call for hunt livery, and you may be asked to snap it.

Spurs are also used on horses who do not respond to the leg aids, either for increase of speed or for movement to one side or the other. Spurs simply increase the effect of the rider's legs. No rider who has not gained complete control of his lower leg should wear spurs, for the constant scraping of spurs against a horse's sides will only excite him and eventually sour him to their use.

There are, of course, many different kinds of spurs, but probably the most popular is the Hunting Spur. This comes in varying lengths of shank and has a rounded knob at the end. It is not very severe and usually is sufficient. Some have little rowels built into the knobs, increasing their severity. Also commonly used is the Prince of Wales Spur, which has no knob and is sometimes more effective. This also comes in varying lengths. Real rowel spurs are very severe and should only be used for schooling, if ever. Because a horse's skin is very thin it is easily cut by the rowels. A schooling with these spurs will not usually wear off in a hurry. Most people never find it necessary to use a rowel spur — it's much too brutal.

42

HORSEMANSHIP

The various bits used on horses are the most complicated of the artificial aids, and we shall leave the discussion of these for a subsequent chapter on equipment, at which point we shall also take up the question of martingales. For the time being we shall assume that your horse has been properly bitted by your instructor, and we shall also leave the use of martingales to his discretion for now.

SUMMARY

The aids are your controls on a horse and you must learn to apply them with great skill, concealing their use. The natural aids are: legs, for increase of speed and movement of the horse's body; hands, for decrease of speed and change of direction by use of direct, indirect, leading, bearing and pulley reins; voice, through tone and inflection; weight, through its placement. The artificial aids are: spurs, to increase the effect of the legs; whips, for forward motion; bits, for control of the horse; martingales, to keep horses' heads low. The artificial aids are designed to augment the effects of the natural aids and should be applied with great care.

CHAPTER VII

Schooling with the Aids

YOUR ABILITY to make your horse respond to the various aids by applying them correctly is the proof of how well you actually ride. If you cannot make your horse respond you are merely a passenger on his back. It is all very well to have a good position on a horse, but if you cannot manage him you will not be very happy or very successful. So until your position is good and you are really secure on a horse you should ride horses which you can easily manage. On these horses you can learn to apply the aids at the same time you are learning position. Everything you do or *don't* do on your horse is going to school him or sour him, so you must learn the importance of discipline from the very beginning.

A horse will get away with anything he can — "give him an inch and he'll take a mile" is really true. While it is necessary to understand his fears and temperament, then, it is equally important to discipline him strictly if he is to work for you and not against you. Discipline is schooling, and a good rider can not only ride schooled horses, but he can school a green or soured horse. The way to school a horse is with punishment and reward, and the aids are our means of punishment. Reward is the lack of punishment.

Punishment is the application of the aids; reward is the lack of the aids, or the relaxation of them. So to punish or reward your horse, you must have perfect control of the aids, and good co-ordination. You must apply the aids when you want your horse to do something, and you must not relax the aids until he has completely obeyed you; then you relax them completely. This way your horse will learn that it is better to obey you immediately and be rewarded than to resist you, hoping that you will change your mind. First decide exactly what you want your horse to do, then give him the *correct* command. If he does not obey, increase the pressure or severity of your aids, resorting to a crop or spurs if necessary. But once you start something, you *must* finish it. It is very important to be consistent, so never give up. Insist that he obey you.

Your first use of the aids will be for increase and decrease of speed. When you

44

want your horse to move forward, you relax the reins and use your legs. When you want him to stop, you relax your legs and use your reins. It's as simple as that, but because horses sometimes do not respond readily to these aids, it is necessary for you to school them until they do respond. The way to school them is a simple exercise called trotting and stopping.

First you establish contact with the horse's mouth by taking up any slack in your reins so that he will feel any pressure you exert on the reins. Then you ask him to move into a slow trot, or sitting trot, by applying pressure with your legs. When he trots, relax your legs. After he has trotted for several strides, exert pressure on your reins to make him halt, increasing the pressure until he has obeyed you by stopping completely. It is a good idea to use your voice as well by saying sharply, "Whoa," at the same time that you first ask him to stop. When he has obeyed your command, relax your hands completely. This is his reward. Count to three slowly, then prepare to trot again. If he should try to move before you have finished the count, bring him back quickly with your reins and count again. He should stand perfectly still for these few seconds. Trot and stop at the slow trot until he has learned to halt quickly and stand quietly. Do not stop him at the same point on the ring each time, for he will associate stopping with that particular place instead of with your command. Eventually, he will learn to halt at your voice command of "Whoa." By sitting at the slow trot you will keep him from breaking into a full trot by your weight as well as your reins. The pace should be about six miles per hour.

When he has learned to obey at the slow trot, do the same thing at a full trot. You will probably have to apply more pressure to the reins to make him stop as you are asking for a greater decrease. The important thing is not to relax any pressure on the reins until he has come to a complete stop, but the moment he obeys, you must relax the pressure completely. This is how he learns to associate obedience with reward.

Trotting and stopping should be done for at least five or ten minutes every day on any horse. It is good schooling for you and your horse in the use of the aids and response to them. It is also excellent for limbering you both up. It is good for mouthing a horse, particularly a green one, as it makes the horse's mouth more sensitive to your commands so that it will require less and less pressure on it. But most important is the fact that it will teach your horse to respect your commands and that you will reward him when he deserves it.

When your horse has learned to trot and stop well, you may also canter and stop. When you do this, keep the pace of your canter fairly slow, but do not let him break into a trot. After he has stopped for the count of three, back him three steps, and move him out into the canter from his position after backing. This is excellent schooling for a horse who does not depart into the canter well, because it collects him completely, which is the way he should be before breaking into the canter. When you have accomplished this at the canter you will have a horse who is well schooled for ring work, one who will never get out of control, and one on whom you will always look smooth.

Another very important exercise for ring work is bending. When a horse bends around a turn or in a circle, he moves his whole body in the arc of the turn, rather than bulging his barrel in toward the center of the ring or circle. Any horse who does not bend is not at all well schooled, and it is immediately evident to both the rider and the onlooker.

BENDING
The rider bends his horse's body around a turn by using an indirect rein in front of the withers and a strong leg on the inside of the turn.

In making a horse bend around a corner or a circle the lateral aids are used — that is, the leg and rein aids are both applied on the same side of the horse. In this case, the inside leg and inside rein are used, while the outside leg and rein remain passive. The particular rein which you will use in this movement is the indirect rein in front of the withers. In turning to the right, you will use your right leg and right indirect rein in front of the withers. This will move his right shoulder and right side toward the left in an arc like that of the turn. If, however, your horse should throw his hindquarters away from the center of the circle, it would be necessary to use your outside leg to keep him in the circle. On a corner, the rail automatically prevents his hindquarters from flying out.

The same aids which you use in bending a horse are used to prevent him from cutting corners or throwing his hindquarters in toward the center of the ring. For these you will have to use a stronger leg than you will in bending. These aids are also used to keep a horse close to the rail in a ring, for he should never be allowed to wander away from the rail, even in preparing for the canter.

If your horse does not at first respond to bending, work him in very small circles which will practically force him to bend, using the aids at the same time. As he responds, make the circles larger and larger until he is bending all the way around the ring.

Any horse you work with should also be taught to flex, if he does not already know how. When a horse is flexed, his neck is bent at the crest and his chin is tucked in toward his chest slightly. This relaxes both his neck and his jaw, which makes him respond more readily to the rein aids. When he is flexed he cannot resist the rein aids by stiffening his jaw and he is always on the bit. Saddle horses flex very easily, but hunters, who often carry their heads rather low and their noses forward, have to be schooled constantly to flex.

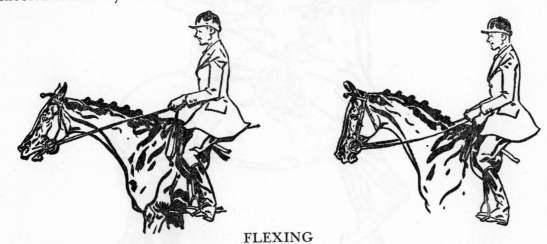

FLEXING

1. Even pressure is applied on the reins and with the legs until . . .
2. the horse relaxes his jaw, dropping his chin and bending his neck, causing a slack in the reins, which is his reward.

Making a horse flex is not difficult though it may take some time before he will respond readily to this command. At a standstill establish contact with your horse's mouth by taking up any slack in the reins until you can feel his mouth. Then, increasing the pressure on his mouth sufficiently to keep him at a standstill, apply pressure to his sides with your legs. The pressure with the reins and the legs should be equalized so that he will neither move forward nor backward. Hold this pressure until he drops his chin in toward his chest, and then relax all pressure. The movement of his chin will be very slight, but the moment you feel it you must reward it immediately. You will feel it and see it in a momentary slackening of the reins. After he has learned it at a standstill, try it at the walk. Eventually, you will be able to keep him flexed at the various gaits. This is how you keep him on the bit all the time you are working. This is a particularly important exercise for horses who are "disconnected," or move their front and hindquarters independently of one another. Riding a disconnected horse feels like what one would imagine riding an eel would be like, every part moving in a different direction. Flexing pulls a horse together so that he feels strong and compact under you and makes him more alert and responsive to all the aids.

BACKING — INCORRECTLY

The rider attempts to outweigh her horse with pressure on the reins alone, causing the horse to throw his head up and to back unevenly, if at all.

BACKING — CORRECTLY

1. The rider first flexes his horse with even pressure on the reins and with his legs.
2. Increasing the pressure on the reins the rider commands the horse to move backwards in even steps.

Backing a horse is just like flexing, though most people do not seem to be aware of this. Most riders, in trying to back their horses, simply haul on their mouths until they have outweighed their horses so that they will move backwards. When this method is used, the horse usually takes one or two uncertain steps backward, placing his feet out toward the sides. Certainly this is not right, for a horse should move backward as well as he moves forward, in even steady steps. To back correctly you halt your horse, apply pressure on the reins and with your legs, flexing your horse. Then you increase the pressure on his mouth until he has taken three or four steps back. If he should swing his hindquarters out to one side or the other, you simply apply more leg pressure on the side toward which he is moving. Any horse is a little afraid of moving backward because he is never quite sure what is behind him, so your commands must be very steady and sure. The moment he has backed, relax all pressure

49

as a reward. When teaching a young or green horse to back, you should only ask him to back one or two steps at a time, then relax the rein pressure but hold the leg pressure until he moves forward. Move him forward several steps before asking him to back again, for he can very easily be soured by the constant pressure of legs and reins.

Another command which nearly every rider gives incorrectly is the command to canter. The most common method is the use of lateral aids. That is, outside leg and outside rein. This is usually taught as, "pull his head to the rail and kick with your outside leg." This is effective because it puts the horse's weight on his outside front foot leaving his inside foot free to take the correct lead. But it doesn't look very nice, twisting his head to the rail and throwing his hindquarters in toward the center of the ring, so that he is at a forty-five degree angle. A horse should remain parallel to the rail as he departs into the canter, and the way to do it is very simple. Diagonal aids are used. That is, the rider uses the *inside* rein and the outside leg. The rein which is used is the indirect rein in front of the withers on the inside, placing his weight on the outside front foot so that he will lead with his inside front foot. The rider's outside leg is used for forward motion and to prevent the horse from bending his body away from the inside rein, keeping his body absolutely straight. This is particularly important when cantering and changing leads on a straight line or in cantering a figure eight, where it is necessary to keep your horse straight between the two circles where you change leads.

When cantering to the right, you should be on the right lead, which means the horse leads with his right front foot, his inside foot. When cantering to the left, you should be on the left lead. If a horse canters around a turn on the wrong lead, he will have to cross his legs which will, naturally, have unpleasant effects — namely, stumbling or falling down.

If you should be asked to canter on a false lead, you should take the wrong lead on purpose, by using the opposite aids. If you are traveling to the right, you will ask for the left lead by using the outside indirect rein in front of the withers and the inside leg. For the left lead, then, you use the left rein and right leg. For the right lead, you use the right rein and left leg.

Should you be on a horse who will not take the correct lead you can school him by cantering him in circles on the wrong lead, making the circles smaller and smaller until he either changes his lead himself or falls down. Repeat this until he has learned to take the correct lead. It may take a long time to school him, but sometimes perseverance is your only weapon. The reason a horse will consistently refuse to take a certain lead is usually because he is a little sore in one leg and does not like to put his weight on it, or he may never have been taught both leads, as in the case of western horses, who often are never worked in a ring. But a good western horse, like a polo pony, should be able to make flying changes automatically with the change of direction. A flying change is a change of lead in the air, without a stop or even a change of pace.

Collecting your horse by flexing him is very important in the departure into the canter. You should never run a horse into a canter by pushing him into a fast disconnected trot until he has to break into a canter. This not only looks perfectly terrible, but often, if he does take the correct lead in front, he will take the wrong lead behind. The only way to put a horse into a canter is to collect him so that he is all together, so to speak, and then give the correct command. It should and can be so smooth that the onlooker will not even be aware that you are asking him to canter. If you have trouble collecting him for a canter, a very good method for schooling him

TURN ON THE FOREHAND
The horse is pivoting on his left front foot, moving his haunches to the right.

The rider places the horse's weight on his left front foot by using a right indirect rein in front of the withers. He is moving the horse's haunches to the right with a strong left leg. This shows diagonal aids.

51

and yourself is to stop, back three steps, and put him immediately into a canter so that his first forward step after backing is his inside front foot leading into the canter. The fact that this method is so effective is good proof that the horse should be thoroughly collected before he is asked to canter. Even when you want him to break into a canter from a trot, you must collect him at the trot first and then command the canter.

Two more movements which every rider should be able to execute are the turn on the forehand and the turn on the haunches. These are important in teaching you the use of the aids and in schooling your horse to respond to them.

The easier of the two turns is the turn on the forehand. This is actually a pivot on the forelegs. Diagonal aids are used: the indirect rein in front of the withers on

TURN ON THE HINDQUARTERS
The horse is pivoting on his left hind foot, moving his forequarters to the left.

The rider places the horse's weight on his left hind foot by using a right indirect rein behind the withers. He is moving the horse's forequarters to the left with a strong right leg. This shows lateral aids.

52

the side toward which you want your horse's haunches to move, and the leg on the opposite side. If you wish to move your horse's hindquarters to the right you use the right indirect rein in front of the withers, placing his weight on his left front leg, which is the leg he will pivot on, leaving the right front leg free to move around. Then you use your left leg to push his haunches toward the right. You must hold your contact with the left rein also, however, to prevent your horse from moving forward. Too much pressure on both reins will cause him to move backwards. For a turn to the left, or clockwise, you use your left indirect rein and right leg.

For the turn on the haunches, lateral aids are used: the indirect rein in *back* of the withers and the leg on the opposite side from that toward which you want his forehand to move. That is, for a turn to the right, or clockwise, you use the left rein and left leg. For a turn to the left, you use the right rein and leg. Here, again, it is important to hold your contact with the horse's mouth so that he will not move forward as he turns. The indirect rein in back of the withers serves to place the horse's weight on his hind leg on the opposite side, so that leg may be used as a pivot and the other is free to move.

Whenever you are working your horse you should include all of the movements and exercises we have mentioned. These are good for keeping your horse supple and in schooling him and yourself to the use of the aids. You should also work him in circles and figure eights, and changes of direction diagonally across the ring. Your first five minutes of work should be spent in walking your horse; then trot him in both directions, making circles and half circles from the rail. Then you should canter him in both directions, and perhaps give him a short hand gallop, but let him walk for a few minutes between each change of gait. You should also back your horse a few times every day, at various intervals during the exercising. Backing is not something that should be done only in the show ring. You should stand and flex him, as this is very good for mouthing him, or educating his mouth. You should turn him on his forehand and haunches, so that he will be flexible and responsive. But of all these, trotting is the best work for a horse as it is not tiring and "muscles him up" and gets off fat, putting him in good working condition, which is the way a horse should be kept.

SUMMARY

It is very important that your horse be strongly disciplined at all times, and the best way to achieve this is through reward and punishment. Application of the aids is punishment, and reward is lack of punishment. Make your commands clear to your horse and insist on his obeying. A good way to school him to the use of the aids is trotting and stopping. Exercises which are important for both horse and rider are: bending in corners, flexing, backing correctly, turn on the forehand using diagonal aids, turn on the haunches using lateral aids. For a canter the horse must be well collected through flexing, and diagonal aids should be used to break him into the canter.

CHAPTER VIII

Outwitting Your Horse

OUR GREATEST ADVANTAGE over horses is our intelligence, though too few riders make use of it. It is certainly easier to outwit so large and strong an animal than to outlast him. Horses are very easily managed when they are ridden cleverly, but once a horse gets out of hand his tremendous strength puts the rider at a distinct disadvantage. The point is to keep him in hand by keeping him relatively happy and calm. You should never get your horse excited by asking too much of him — do everything gradually. Nor should the aids be used severely unless absolutely necessary. A great kick in the ribs or jab on the mouth of any horse will provoke him to anger and steady pressure with legs or reins on a sensitive horse will infuriate him and cause unpleasant results. If you are using a curb rein, for example, you must take advantage of its severity only when you have to, for steady pressure on this rein will invariably cause a light-mouthed horse to run in an effort to get away from the pain of the bit. In fact, this is the cause of most runaways. You must remember that your equipment is very severe and should always be handled with care.

You cannot master a horse with your body alone. A body without a mind is like a car without a driver — it can't go anywhere. If only a body were needed to ride a horse, monkeys could ride, though looking at some riders, it would indeed seem that that were the case. Too many people try to ride without using their heads.

When you are on a horse you have to be able to make instantaneous decisions, and they have to be the right decisions. Every move your horse makes must be aided or countered by action on your part. You have to know when to assist him and when to oppose him, and how. It takes years to learn to make the right decision immediately in any given instance, and even then, a mistake is easily made. You have to use psychology with horses, and this psychology is based on common sense — "horse sense." Experience is your best teacher. That is why people need instructors when they are learning how to ride, so they can profit from the experience of their teachers and eventually learn how to use their own judgment. You have to learn from experience how your horse will react to your actions and how you should react to his.

You have to be able to think quickly and act quickly, to make split-second decisions.

Your mind can also work against you, especially in the case of beginners, in the form of fear. The timid rider must, of course, overcome his fear before he can really learn to ride. But in the hands of a competent horseman, in whom he has confidence, the timid rider, too, can achieve greater things than he may have imagined possible. The mere fact that he has confidence in his instructor will enable him to prove to himself that he need not be afraid.

Frightened riders cause their own accidents. A fairly able rider, for example, may be cantering along when his horse stumbles, or simply increases his speed. This inexperienced rider imagines that the horse has tried to buck or is going to run away, so he tightens his reins and squeezes his legs against his horse's sides in an effort to gain security. The horse is confused by this and because of the leg pressure increases his pace. The rider becomes more frightened, freezes every muscle in his body and, therefore, cannot sit his horse any longer, and freezes on the reins so the horse fights the bit. This all results in frightening the horse until he really does do something. Eventually the rider falls off, of course, and probably thinks it all was the horse's fault.

A really good rider has no fear, and anyone without fear can become a really good rider after he has had experience *if* he learns to use his head. And a really good rider, incidentally, is one who can climb up on any horse and ride and school him, who can feel a horse's mouth and know what kind of bit to put on him, who can plan the schooling and development of a young or green horse. He is someone who can make the right decisions and enforce them. Most fine riders have had, during their first few years, the advantage of a good "ground man," someone who could make the right decisions and let the rider enforce them. This is invaluable and takes years off the time it takes to learn these things. It teaches the rider to use common sense, which, unfortunately, is not very common.

There are two principles of psychology which you should use when working with horses. First is "anticipation," second is "attention diversion."

Anticipation is simply knowing what your horse is going to do before he does it, and thereby preventing it. You have to learn virtually to think like a horse. Imagine yourself in those four shoes and decide what you would do if you were he. If you see someone in a bright coat leaning on the rail of the ring, for instance, you must realize that your horse will probably not see the coat until he is nearly there, and then, being close to it, he will probably be frightened. When a horse is frightened, he shies away from that which is frightening him. So you prepare for him to shy. Should you tighten your reins and squeeze your legs against him so that you will be more secure and not fall off? No indeed. You simply sit there *calmly*, taking up your reins so that there is no slack in them, giving him confidence with your feel of his mouth, pushing him up on the bit so that he can't duck away. You might use your voice to calm him so that he will not be afraid. If he does try to shy as he passes the coat you use a stronger leg on the side opposite the object in order to keep him in line. If the object is on the left, you use the right leg and, if necessary, a stronger right rein. If you tighten up on him suddenly as you see the object, he will think that he should be afraid, and if he hasn't thought of shying, you have put the idea into his mind. You must be relaxed but prepared.

Anticipation is also feeling. If you are trotting, for example, and you feel your horse lengthening his stride and missing the exact cadence of the trot, you know that he is going to try to break into a canter. Don't let a moment pass, for he may break during that moment. Immediately close your hands, increasing the pressure on his mouth and bringing him back to a steady, collected trot. Or while you are cantering you may feel the slightest decrease of pace, or perhaps no evident decrease of pace but simply a "disconnected" feeling because your horse is no longer collected in his stride and is missing the exact cadence of the canter. This calls for more legs immediately. Not a kick, but a squeeze with the legs, collecting him with your reins at the same time. You must keep him on the bit with steady rein pressure and even greater leg pressure. You must learn to feel the movement of every muscle in his body through your legs and hands. Then you will be able to feel any deviation from the proper stride and cadence of his gait and prevent his breaking into another gait.

Sometimes anticipation is a combination of thought and feeling at the same time. If you are approaching a bridge, for instance, you may realize that your horse may not want to cross it and at the same time feel his reluctance and perhaps a slackening of his pace and a side to side movement of his head as he looks for some place to go as he ducks away from the bridge. Here, again, you must drive him up on the bit with your legs while holding a steady pressure with your hands, calming him at the same time, as he is probably afraid. As you drive him up on the bit, however, always be sure that the rein pressure is no greater than he requires, *i.e.* no greater than that which is necessary simply to keep the slack out of the reins. With this slight pressure, remember, your hands must give and take as his mouth requires. Since a horse's head moves slightly forward and back as he moves, this light feel must increase and decrease. As his head moves forward, your hands must give, ever so slightly, and as his chin moves back, the pressure must increase. It will take a long time to perfect this feeling with your hands, and certainly the great majority of riders never do achieve this perfection, but you must strive constantly to have good hands. This give and take does not requires any movement of the hands themselves, only of the last two fingers, which open and close to decrease and increase pressure.

The second principle of psychology with a horse, attention diversion, is most often overlooked by inexperienced riders. Experienced riders, if they have not been taught it, usually come to find it by themselves, necessity being the mother of invention.

They find it necessary when a horse refuses to do something to approach it from another angle, psychologically, which is what attention diversion is. When a child refuses to surrender a toy you simply interest him in something else, and while he is engrossed with that, you pick up the toy. The same method is used with horses. When they refuse to do something, divert their attention to something else, and while they are concerned with that, you make them do what they had formerly refused.

Imagine, for example, that you have a horse who will not cross a stream. As you approach it he starts to snort and hesitates in his gait, moving a little in one direction, then a little way in the other direction. Finally you leg him up to the edge of the stream and he stands with his toes at the very edge of it, sniffing it and snorting at it. Then he dips one toe into the water, as if to check the temperature, decides he doesn't like it, and withdraws his foot. Even though you are using your legs and driving him up on the bit, he won't go into the stream, he just moves a little from side to side. Then you use a crop on him, but it doesn't do any good, it just gets him more excited and frightened. He's half afraid of the stream, especially if the sunlight is making strange shadows in it, and he half wants to play. You just can't force him into it, no matter what you do. This is where you use attention diversion.

Turn his head to one side, depending on which side has the most space, and turn him in that direction, taking a few steps forward. Then use the opposite rein and lots of leg, turning him quickly into the stream, and once in it, keep him moving with legs and crop, keeping a feel of his mouth at the same time. If you don't get him into the stream at the first try, turn him in the opposite direction and then turn him quickly into the stream. This method of turning first in one direction then the other and then into the stream nearly always works, unless the horse is genuinely afraid of the water. If he is really frightened, it may be necessary the first time to dismount and lead him into it, which is not very good for one's boots and should, therefore, only be done as a last resort. Once you have got your horse through the stream you should immediately remount and ride him back and forth through it until he has no fear or illusions about what it is. Most horses actually like the feel of water around their feet. In fact, if your horse should start pawing and try to get his head down while you are in the stream, watch out — he wants to lie down in it. Get him out of it in a hurry. That's one reason why you should never let your horse drink when you are crossing a stream. The other good reason is that he is probably quite warm from being ridden and the cold water would be very harmful to him.

I had one mare who would never walk directly into a stream, no matter what I did, so after turning her in one direction and then in the other, I would have to move her into the stream sideways, using my leg and an indirect rein on the side away from the stream. Once she was in it I could straighten her out and she would walk freely through it.

58

HORSEMANSHIP

Sometimes in the ring, when a horse is lined up with other horses he will be reluctant to leave the line when you want to move him out onto the rail. In this case, again, you may reach your goal by the same devious method of moving him a step or two to the side before going forward. If you just sit there and kick him, even though you have put him on the bit, you may stand there for days without moving. Horses can be very stubborn.

On the other hand, horses also try to use the same methods of attention diversion on their riders, and though the riders are supposed to have more sense, they often fall victim to it. If you ask your horse to do something he doesn't want to do, he will try to get your mind off your goal by playing around until you've either forgotten or given up what you wanted in the first place. Be sure this doesn't happen. Always finish whatever you start out to do.

If you want to go to a certain point and your horse ducks around to the left, for instance, don't think you are being clever if you keep on turning to the left until you have completed a circle and he is going in the direction you originally wanted. He's winning if you do this, and in another few steps he'll duck to the left again. Even if he ducks all the way around until he's facing the direction you've wanted, you must retrace the steps by turning him to the right and making him go in the right direction. If he ducks to the left, use that right rein, and don't give up for an instant until he has obeyed you. Once he's started toward the left he's going to try awfully hard to keep going in that direction, and it's going to be very difficult to get him to turn to the right. You may have to shorten your right rein until you're practically holding his bit in your hand, but you must use the right rein. If he's trying to turn to the right, you must use your left rein. Very recently on a trail ride a rider let her horse make one circle to the left and he kept on circling and wouldn't straighten out. Finally I persuaded her to use her right rein, though she thought it was ridiculous, and he straightened out. But the damage had been done. For the rest of the ride his head kept wagging from side to side, and every few steps he would duck to the left, each time with more force than the time before, until he was finally too strong for his rider and I had to mount this usually docile animal and school him myself, and not without some difficulty, for a disobedience unpunished becomes a major vice rapidly. Once a horse has won a point he'll keep hammering at it until he has got his way and is heading for the stable at a good clip. Never, never give in to a horse.

A major vice which is not uncommon, being caused most often by the rider himself, is rearing. Many horses just never think of rearing, while it is often the first misdeed to occur to others. The few horses who rear with malice, standing high upon their hind feet and pawing the air with their front feet, are not, of course, the result of poor riding. They are ornery. But the many horses you see raising their front feet three to four feet from the ground are almost always the result of riders

59

who clash their aids. That is, the rider applies constant pressure with his legs (and you often see them wearing spurs, too) while allowing the horse no forward motion because of his tight hold on the reins. The horse has nowhere to go but up. I know one fairly good rider who sold one horse because of his constant rearing and bold way of going and bought another; in two months she had the same problem as a result of her constant legs and heavy hands.

When a horse rears you should have one immediate reaction: put your hands forward. If you move your hands toward his mouth you will not pull on it, causing him to lose his balance and fall over backwards, landing on you. If you lose your own balance your hands will come back and you will inevitably pull the horse over on you. Your second reaction should be to use your legs. The horse's weight is on his hind legs as a result of your hands so you should use the opposite aid, your legs, to push him forward, putting his weight forward and making him move forward so that he will have to come down in front. If you happen to have a crop in your hand it should be used with force on his hindquarters, which will make him jump quickly forward. If you have a horse that habitually rears, you should realize first that you are most likely doing something wrong. Further, you should carry a crop on him so that you will be able to punish him well when he rears, giving him his head at the same time. The best cure for rearing is one that we do not suggest you try. It is turning a horse over by pulling hard on the reins once he is standing up, thus causing him to lose his balance and fall hard on his back, the rider escaping just before the horse crashes to the ground. This may sound rather severe for both horse and rider, but the outlaw horses who respond to nothing else deserve no less than this to frighten them so that they will be afraid of rearing. It's a pretty sure cure but not very pleasant for the rider in that split second before the horse lands.

Bucking seldom reaches the proportion of a major vice, but is a bothersome minor one. As with rearing, it should be anticipated and prevented whenever possible. To buck, a horse must get his head down, so you must keep it up where it belongs. But once he has got his head down and is bucking, you must jerk his head up immediately by pulling hard on one rein. Once you have got his head up, keep it up. As you pull his head up you should also use your legs to make him move forward, for a horse bucks in one spot and usually keeps his legs very stiff, just to make the concussion greater for the rider. If you make him move forward he will have to bend his legs and move out of the buck.

Some horses kick. Any horse will kick if another horse gets too close to him from behind and steps on his heels or bites his rump. But some horses look for horses to come near them so that they can kick. When this is the case, your only weapon is vigilance. You must be constantly aware of every horse within ten feet of your horse, and you must keep your horse moving forward at every moment, for he has to stop to kick. If you are riding next to someone, you must keep your horse's head turned toward the other horse, for if his head is toward the other horse, his tail can't be, so he can't kick. When a horse does kick with you, however, you must use your crop on him severely as punishment and set him back hard on his haunches with a strong rein.

There are some horses who kick when they are cantering or as they land after a fence, or even over the middle of a fence. These horses have been virtually taught to kick by riders who used their legs constantly and who, when jumping, squeezed their lower legs tightly against the horses' sides. If you squeeze your legs against your horse in an effort to gain greater security you will first cause him to quicken his pace, and eventually irritate him to the point of kicking out whenever he feels the added pressure. If you have a horse who kicks out while jumping or landing you have no recourse but to take great care in applying any leg pressure, consciously or unconsciously, and keep his head up as he lands.

If you have a horse who kicks out while he is cantering, as at the end of a ring during a course of jumps, your goal should be to keep his weight on his hindquarters so that he cannot kick out. If you always keep his head a little higher than you ordinarily would and with strong reins keep his weight on his haunches, you will be able to prevent his kicking. In order to kick out he must put his head down and put all his weight on his front feet while he throws his hindquarters high into the air, so whenever you feel this coming, you must pull his head up and force his weight onto his hind feet. This is also true of a horse who kicks out at other horses, but while the use of a crop punishes the horse who kicks with malice a crop must not be used on the horse who kicks out from extreme leg pressure, for instead of punishing him it only increases the cause of his anger.

Something which is not really a vice but an unpleasant nuisance is boring on the bit. This usually occurs in horses with heavy necks, large heads or mutton withers. A horse who bores on the bit is constantly putting his head down low and pushing his nose forward, pulling the rider out of the saddle in an effort to get a completely free rein. Such a horse must be carefully bitted, the best for this usually being some type of snaffle, for this bit works upon the bars of the mouth and also the lips and tends to bring a horse's head up more than any other bit. When riding such a horse you must take care to keep his head up by little jerks on the reins whenever you feel a dead weight in your hands. Once he gets his head down, you must jerk very hard on one rein in order to get his head up again, and once it is up, you must keep moving your fingers on the reins to keep the bit moving about in his mouth.

Strict discipline with your horse will reward you with a well-mannered mount. If, however, your horse finds out he can get away with a number of minor things he will eventually try to get rid of you or to run away. Of course a "runaway" can also result from a sudden fright which causes the horse to shy and then run. If you should find your horse really out of control ever, you should first try the pulley rein — this generally works well. If the pulley rein does not work, try this: as the horse is galloping put both your hands on one rein, as close to the mouth as possible, and pull with all your strength on that one rein. This will pull his head around so that he will have to turn and thus slow down for fear of falling. If you happen to have the presence of mind, you might look to see what lead he is galloping on and pull the opposite rein. If he is on the left lead, for example, pull on the right rein, for this will increase the effectiveness of the turn since he is greatly handicapped in trying to turn on the wrong lead. This method is hardly good horsemanship, but occasionally emergencies do arise, and if you know you have a sure way to stop a horse you will have less fear.

SUMMARY

Our intelligence is our greatest advantage over horses so we should make the best use of it. You must use your head all the time you are on a horse and be ready to make quick decisions and carry them through. You must not have fear — there is no need for it and it does great harm. Fear freezes a rider's muscles and well as his mind, frightens the horse, and causes accidents. When working with horses you must use simple psychology by: anticipation, feeling what a horse is going to do next and preventing it; attention diversion, taking his mind off that which he refuses to do and making him do it while he is concerned with something else. Never give in to your horse — always make him do what you want.

CHAPTER IX

Care of the Horse

A VERY IMPORTANT PART of learning how to ride is learning all about the proper care of the horse and his equipment. When the occasion arises you should be capable of tacking and untacking your horse, grooming him and even feeding him. You should know how to adjust bridles and saddles for yourself, or to check their adjustment if someone else has tacked your horse for you. A good groom is worth his weight in gold these days, and if you are fortunate enough to have a good one, you can learn a lot from him. More likely your groom is pretty green, though, and it is you who will have to teach him, for you are supposed to know these things.

"Tack" is the general name given to all articles of equipment, such as bridles, saddles, martingales, breastplates, and so forth. Both the leather and the metal should be kept immaculately clean at all times, and should be cleaned before and after each use. Bits should be washed after each use, and all the metal should be polished periodically with metal polish. The leather should be washed with a warm, damp sponge and saddle or glycerine soap every day. It should be sponged on both sides, and at least once a week all buckles and keepers should be undone so the leather under them can be kept supple and clean.

There are three basic types of bits: snaffle, Pelham and double, each having a different effect on a horse's mouth. The plain snaffle is the least severe bit and is effective primarily through pressure on the horse's lips when the reins are pulled. Slightly more severe is the twisted snaffle, which is the same as the plain snaffle except that the bars are beveled, making a sharper surface in the horse's mouth. The most severe snaffle is the wire snaffle which has double bars made of heavy twisted wire coming to two sharp points on either side of the center of the bit. The wire snaffle strongly affects the roof of the horse's mouth as well as the lips and is a very effective bit. Snaffle bits have a single rein which is attached to the large rings on either side of the bit.

A Pelham bit affects primarily the bars, or ridges, of the roof of the mouth, and secondarily, the lips. There are two reins, one the snaffle rein, which is attached to

63

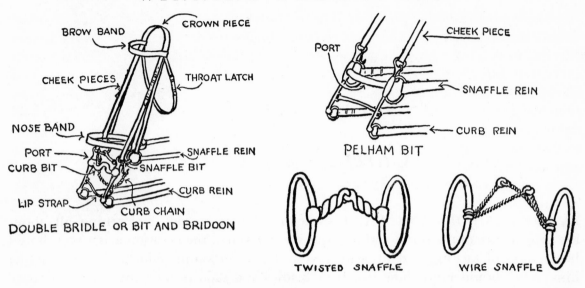

the top ring and exerts pressure on the lips, and the other, the curb rein, which is attached to the lower ring. The lower ring is at the bottom of the shank or branch of the bit, and by leverage, pressure on the curb rein forces the port, or the bar of the bit which is in the horse's mouth, against the roof of the horse's mouth. There is a curb chain on this bit which is attached on either side of the bit and lies under the horse's chin. The tighter the curb chain, the greater the leverage and the more severe the bit becomes.

The severity of the Pelham bit also depends upon the shape of the port and the length of the shank. The higher the port is in the center, the greater is the pressure on the bars of the horse's mouth. The longer the shank is, the greater is the leverage which forces the port against the bars of the mouth. A long-shanked, high-ported Pelham is an extremely severe bit, and used more on saddle horses than on hunters. A short-shanked, plain-ported Pelham, on the other hand is a very nice bit, the shortest of these being the Tom Thumb, which has about a two-and-a-half inch shank and is used commonly on hunters and jumpers with good mouths. The advantage of this over a snaffle is that it serves to bring a horse's chin in and to flex him so that the bit is more effective. It also often helps to bring a horse's head down if he carries it too high.

The double bridle, or bit and bridoon, is two separate bits in one bridle. It is made up of a small snaffle bit and a curb bit, and is similar in appearance to the Pelham. The snaffle has its own rein and works as any other snaffle. The curb bit is like the Pelham except that it has no upper ring, only the one on the end of the shank and usually has a high port, for it may be used or left alone, since the two bits are separate. The Tom Thumb double is also a very good bit for hunters and jumpers and helps to bring a horse's head up if he tends to bore against the bit. A long-shanked double bridle is probably the most common bit found on saddle horses as it is very effective in making a horse flex. This bit, when properly used, can regulate a horse's every step, but extreme care must be used by the rider in manipulating the reins at all times. Constant pressure on the curb can irritate a horse tremendously and either ruin his mouth or drive him to extreme disobedience, such as running away. Too tight a curb chain is also very dangerous and can cause the horse to refuse to move forward or to rear and even turn over backwards. When the curb chain is properly adjusted the shank of the curb can be freely moved backwards to a forty-five degree angle from the perpendicular. When the shank is moved further back than that by pressure on the reins the horse will react immediately. If the curb chain is so loose that the shank can be moved freely any further back, the curb will be ineffective. This is true of the adjustment of the curb chain on a Pelham also.

A snaffle should be adjusted so that, without pressure on the reins, there is one slight wrinkle in the horse's lip. The snaffle of a double bridle may be adjusted more tightly, causing two wrinkles, depending on the need for keeping his head up. A Pelham should be adjusted so that there are no wrinkles in the horse's mouth, but no space between the lip and the bit. The curb of a double bridle should be below the snaffle, about half an inch or so, far enough down in his mouth so that it will not interfere with the snaffle.

On any type of bridle the noseband should not be too tight, nor should the throat latch, and there should be room for your hand between the throat latch and his throat after it has been buckled.

One other bridle you should know about is the hackamore, which does not affect a horse's mouth at all. This has a band across the horse's nostrils and pressure on the reins cuts off his wind. It is not generally acceptable, but may be used in extreme cases where a horse's mouth is too hard, or calloused, to react to a bit, or where a horse's mouth is too sensitive for any bit at all. When improperly used, this can be a brutal bridle and will result in an erratic performance. But if it is very skillfully used by the lightest hands it can bring very good results. If it is used by a rider who at any time needs to rely on his reins for support or balance, such as in the middle of a fence, it can bring disastrous results.

Martingales are used, when necessary, to keep a horse's head from flying up and back. The two common types of martingales are the standing and the running. The standing martingale is attached to the noseband of the bridle and the girth of the saddle. It should be adjusted so that it is long enough to allow the horse to raise his head until it is on a level with his withers. If it is shorter it is too confining, and if it is longer it is ineffective.

The running, or ring martingale is attached to the snaffle reins and the girth, and

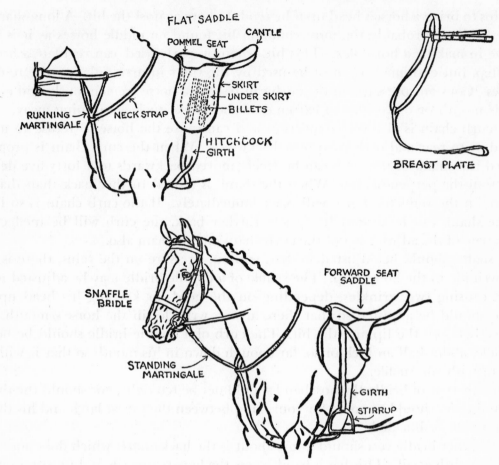

the adjustment is about the same. The standing martingale is used on horses who habitually carry their heads high. The running martingale is used more often on horses who throw their heads up when pressure is applied on the reins. Since it is attached to the snaffle reins, any pressure on these reins works to bring the horse's head down.

There is one other kind of martingale, the Irish martingale, which is a short strap with two rings which are attached to the snaffle reins, causing a bridge between them. When a horse throws his head very high this bridge keeps the reins below the horse's jaws, but it is not particularly effective and is very seldom used.

The two major types of saddles are the flat saddle and the forward-seat saddle. The flat saddle is used most widely for all kinds of work, but the forward-seat saddle is becoming more and more popular for jumping and hunting. The major difference is that the forward-seat saddle has leather padding and rolls in front of the rider's knees, under the skirt of the saddle usually. Also it usually has a higher cantle and

66

allows more room for a very bent knee, whereas the skirt of the flat saddle is cut nearly straight down from the pommel. For jumping, the forward-seat saddle affords more security, but care must be taken that the rider does not come to depend upon those knee-rolls for his security in the saddle. One should be able to jump in a flat saddle as well as a forward-seat saddle.

When putting a saddle on a horse it should be put on from the left side. Place it first on his withers and slide it down onto his back so that you will not get it too far back. The girth should fall just behind his elbow and should be as tight as possible, but not so tight as to wrinkle his flesh, for this would cause it to rub and cause a sore which is difficult to heal if the horse is being used every day. The underneath part of the saddle should be perfectly clean, for if there is any dirt on it it will cause a saddle sore which is also hard to heal. If a horse has thin skin or a sensitive back a sheepskin or felt saddle pad should be used. The most important point, however, is that there is adequate room between the pommel of the saddle and the horse's withers, for when a rider is in the saddle it comes down closer to his withers and if the saddle rubs the withers it will cause a bad sore and bruise the horse. If there is any question, use a pommel pad over his withers. This can be made of sheepskin, or be a knitted pad, or even a folded rub-rag.

When putting a bridle on a horse, first put the reins over his head, then take off his halter. Then, holding the crown of the bridle in your right hand as you stand at the left of his head, slip the bridle up his face, putting his nose in the noseband, holding the bit in your left hand. When the bit is near his mouth, slip it against his teeth, moving it slightly until he opens his mouth. When he opens his mouth, pull the bridle all the way up, putting the bit in his mouth and putting the crown of the bridle over his ears, left first, then the right. If he will not open his mouth, use your thumb and second finger to open it by putting them just inside his mouth in the space between the incisors and the tushes, or "bit teeth," squeezing until he opens his mouth enough for the bit. Once the bridle is on, fasten the throat latch and curb chain, if there is one, laying it perfectly flat before hooking it.

Your horse should be thoroughly groomed every morning after his stall has been cleaned out. You should cross-tie him on the stable floor, that is, with one rope attached to each side of his head, so that he cannot turn or swing around. Whenever he is very dirty, use a rubber currycomb first, in a circular motion, and sparing no strength. As the dirt accumulates inside the currycomb hit it hard on a nearby board in order to shake the dirt out. Next, use a stiff dandy brush in brisk, short strokes, brushing with the lay of his coat, not against it, except in very dirty spots where it is necessary to brush back and forth to loosen the hair. You should keep a metal currycomb in your left hand while brushing, so that every few seconds you can rub the brush against the currycomb to get the dirt out of the brush, shaking the dirt out of the currycomb as often as necessary. This gets all the dirt out of his coat. To get the dirt off the surface of his coat, use a soft body brush in long strokes, smoothing the hair at the same time. The body brush should also be cleaned with the metal currycomb. As a finishing touch, use a soft rub-rag to polish his coat all over. Don't forget that he must be cleaned *all over,* and this includes his face, under his belly, and his legs.

For your horse's mane and tail a dandy brush should be used to clean and untangle the hair, doing his tail stroke by stroke, strand by strand until every hair has been separated. At least every other day a mane comb should be used on both mane and tail, and both should be thinned at least once a month. If the mane is unruly, use a damp dandy brush every morning to train it. If one piece hangs on the wrong side, braid it in a thick, heavy braid and leave it that way for about a week on the right side to train it. To thin the mane or tail, comb the hair straight down and take hold of the longest strand. Then comb the rest of the hair upwards, wrap the long strand around the mane comb and pull. This doesn't hurt, but don't take too large a strand at a time. Do this until the mane or tail is the length you want, but be careful not to make it too thin. If your horse has a roached or hog mane, it should be clipped about twice a month, and his ears and whiskers should be clipped at least once a month.

Every time you groom your horse be careful to clean out his feet thoroughly. This is probably the most important part of grooming, and should be done as often as possible. If his feet are not kept clean at all times he may contract thrush, which is a fungus disease caused by damp manure being left caked in the feet, or by standing in a wet, dirty stall. It is very dangerous because it eats away the soft frog of his foot and causes lameness, because the frog is the part that absorbs the concussion of his foot against the ground. Thrush is easily detected because of its foul odor and, if very progressed, the usually well-defined line of the frog will be out of shape. If arrested in time it can be cured with thrush medicine and extreme care, but it takes quite a while before the foot is back to normal.

To clean the foot stand next to your horse's leg, facing the rear, and leaning against his body to shift his weight onto his opposite foot. Then run your hand slowly down his leg and squeeze his tendon until he lifts his foot; then you hold the foot by placing one hand under the hoof, and clean it thoroughly with a hoof pick. Be sure that the hoof pick is not too sharp, and be very careful not to jab the sensitive frog, which is the V-shaped protrusion pointing toward his toe. After you have cleaned his foot until the sole shows you should use hoof dressing all around the hoof and if the inside is dry, hoof oil on the sole and frog.

After you have finished riding you should always walk your horse until he is perfectly cool. If there are still some wet spots, such as under the saddle, rub these dry with a rub-rag, going against the lay of his coat. In the summer, when there is no danger of his catching cold, you may sponge his back with warm water, scraping it dry with a metal scraper, and preferably, walking him dry. You should also sponge around his ears, eyes, and nostrils, and his dock and between his hind legs. If your horse has white stockings you should sponge these clean, using some castile soap if they are particularly dirty or yellow-looking. His mane and tail should be washed occasionally with castile soap also, by rubbing the roots with a dandy brush, soap and warm water. Only mild castile should be used, and care should be taken that both mane and tail are thoroughly dried before the horse is put away.

As for feeding, both the schedule and the menu depend very much upon the horse and his schedule of work. Generally speaking, feedings should be from six in the morning to six at night. This means that as close to six in the morning as possible he should be given his grain. No sooner than an hour after this he should be watered, if he does not have water in his stall, which is the most desirable. Then he should be given his hay, enough to last through the morning, but never more than he will eat. At noontime he should be watered, hayed and grained again. Then in mid-afternoon he should be watered again, and given his hay shortly after, and around five or six his grain. The noon hay should be the smallest amount; the afternoon hay should be given early enough so that he will eat some before the grain comes, but he should have enough to last him into the night. If possible, he should be watered once again at night, particularly in the summer, and he should always be allowed all the water he will drink, except when watered immediately after graining or when hot. Be sure that he has a salt brick in his feed box at all times, for horses need it, particularly in hot weather, and it increases their desire for water. You should never give a horse grain just before he has to work, nor should you ever take him out in the middle of his graining. Neither should you give him a lot of water just before he works, nor just afterward, particularly if he is still hot, though a swallow of water will help to cool him. If he is perfectly cool when you bring him in he may have all the water he wants.

Crushed oats is the best grain to give a horse who is in steady work, or whole oats, though these are not as easily assimilated. According to the horse and the amount of work he is doing, the ration of grain should be from eight to sixteen quarts a day. For horses which must be kept fairly quiet, a sweet-feed mixture of oats, corn, dried molasses and vitamins and minerals may be used. Every horse should be given a bran mash at least twice a week, preferably before a day of rest. This should be made half of grain and half of bran, and may exceed the usual allowance for the meal in quantity, for bran is a "cool" feed, and is, as a laxative, very good for the horse's system, for his coat, and for putting on good fat. The mash should be made with cold water in summer and hot water in winter, and should never be sloppy but only wet enough to make the bran damp enough to join easily with the grain. It should always be given as the evening meal.

When a horse is out of work, due to lameness or sickness particularly, he should be fed half grain and half bran at all times, for grain is a "hot" feed, and gives him great energy which must always be worked off. In this case it is also a good idea to cut down on the noon feed, or cut it out entirely. Bran is also helpful with a horse who is "off his feed," or refuses to eat his food. Grain which is left over from a meal should never be left in the stall, nor should the next meal be put in on top of it. Everything which is not eaten should be removed, and the next feeding made smaller until he has only as much as he will eat. Often it is helpful to add carrots cut in small pieces and even molasses to the grain to coax him back on his feed. If a horse remains off his feed for a period of three days or more it is wise to call a vet, for his teeth may need "floating," or filing, or there may be something else wrong with him.

The amount of hay you should feed also varies with each horse according to his condition and size and work. Generally speaking, he should be hayed three times a day, morning and night in the amount of two or three leaves, or flakes, which are the sections into which the bale is divided, the size of these sections varying with different baling machines. At noon he should be fed slightly less hay. If a horse can use more weight around his barrel and ribs, feed him all the hay he will eat, but never more than he will eat, as this would discourage him and cause him to eat less and less. If a horse is developing a "hay belly," or a fat, low-hanging belly out of proportion to the rest of his body, keep his hay ration down to a minimum, though it is the bulk of his food and he should never be hungry, and feed more bran and grain in compensation. The hay should be properly aged, but should not be a dull-brown color. It should be slightly greenish, but if it is too green it will not be good for him. Moldy hay should never be fed, either, for while a horse will usually refuse to eat moldy hay, if he should be hungry enough to eat it it can cause very bad colic. If the hay is particularly dry and dusty, or if a horse has any sort of a dry cough, the hay should be sprinkled lightly with water after it has been loosened from the tightly packed leaf. It is not generally necessary, however, to loosen the hay before feeding, for a horse will loosen it himself as he eats it. The hay should be of timothy, or timothy combined with clover, and sometimes with alfalfa also, which is sweeter than the others. Good hay will smell sweet, and taste good when you chew on it yourself. If you're the kind of person who likes to pick up a wisp of hay and chew on it while you're around the barn, you might as well get the best hay you can for your horse — you'll enjoy it a lot more than dry, tasteless hay!

A pleasant supplement to your horse's diet is some kind of crunch, which comes in dry, hard, brown chunks and looks untasty, but which is made of feed with vitamins and minerals and is comparable to dog kibble. Horses find it absolutely delicious and a few pieces a day are very good for them. Crunch, carrots, or sometimes apples, are very good for your horse if you want to pamper him a little, while any amount of sugar is bad for him and not as well appreciated.

No matter how humble your own barn may be, there are certain basic requirements which should be met. You should have a separate room, no matter how small, in which to keep your tack and medicines, and if it is large enough, a quantity of hay. The bulk of the hay may be kept in a loft to be dropped down through a hole as needed. You should have a wooden feed bin, *with* a cover so that in the summer flies can't get in, and at night a loose horse can't raid it. The feed bin should be divided into two or three parts, one for grain, one for bran, and preferably one for crunch, salt, or whatever you wish to keep in it. Be sure that the bottom is solid so that rats, mice or chipmunks can't sneak in and slowly deplete your supply. This bin should be kept in a dry spot and the grain must be kept perfectly dry, for otherwise it will easily mold and be most dangerous to your horse. The reason you must always be particularly careful of what your horse gets to eat is that he cannot vomit if he is sick, and anything that he swallows must go right through his intestines. If it is indigestible it will immediately cause some kind of colic, and serious colic can kill your horse. If you should notice your horse breaking into a sweat, looking unhappily at his stomach and leaning or rubbing against the sides of his stall you can be pretty sure that he has colic. It's a very pathetic sight because it makes them absolutely miserable. You should have a mild colic medicine on hand which you should give him immediately with a syringe or even a large spoon. Hold his tongue all the way out of his mouth with your left hand while you pour the medicine down his throat with the other, immediately putting your left hand under his chin, having let go of his tongue, and pushing his head up as high as possible so that he will swallow the medicine and not let it dribble out. The most important thing is to keep him on his feet, though he will want to lie down and if he does he will surely get cast and may never get up again. After giving him the medicine it is a good idea to walk him awhile. If he does not improve, call a vet immediately, for he may need a stronger medicine, or may have something else wrong with him, such as a twisted intestine.

Also in your tack or feed room should be kept your bedding, which is preferably straw, for this is the most comfortable to lie on, and the easiest to clean. In the stall the straw should be well loosened, and banked higher at the walls. Peat moss can also be used, or shavings or sawdust, though the latter two are sometimes dangerous because a horse will sometimes nibble on them as he eats or even pick up a chunk of wood, which will cause agonizing colic and can be very serious. Also, these are not as easily kept clean, and it is usually necessary to clean all the bedding out each morning and put in fresh bedding at night, for when this stuff is dirty it easily cakes into horses' feet and makes it hard to keep the feet clean.

Your tack room should have both hot and cold running water and should be well lighted. You should have racks for both saddles and bridles, as well as a wooden "saddle horse" on which to clean your saddles or to put them when dirty. A large mobile tack hook, with from two to four prongs, should hang from the ceiling just within arm's reach so that bridles can be hung from it while being cleaned and the reins won't scrape across the floor. Dirty bridles should be hung from this until they are cleaned, which should be immediately. Your bridles should be hung up on their own racks after cleaning, with the reins looped over the noseband. Bits should always be rinsed immediately after use and, if necessary, cleaned with steel wool and then metal polish. All your grooming equipment should be kept either in the bottom of the saddle horse or in a separate cabinet or a portable box. All tack-cleaning equipment should also be kept in the saddle horse or cabinet, and the saddle soap should be placed in a small wooden insert so it can be easily rubbed without being held when you are cleaning tack.

You must also have a medicine cabinet in your tack room, and if possible, in a larger stable, a small ice box in which to keep any drugs which must be kept cool or cold. Your medicine chest should hold any medicines which your vet might give you; plenty of sheet cotton and cotton bandages for doing up legs; wool shipping bandages; absorbent cotton for applying medicine; healing oil for small cuts or sores; "bluing" or gentian violet for leg wounds caused by interfering, grabbing or rubbing; liniment for rubbing down sore tendons or muscles and from which to make leg wash for "hot" bandages for the same purpose; white lotion tablets, from which to make white lotion for a cool bandage when there is heat in any part of the leg, or for use on a sore back or on any joint where there is a temperature; bluestone or something comparable for rubbing and burning off proud flesh from cuts on which it might form; mild colic medicine; cough syrup; vaseline for sores; and any other medicines you might accumulate, such as sulfa or penicillin powder or salve, conditioning solution, or even arsenic.

The trouble horses can get themselves into is unlimited, and you must be prepared for anything and everything. We had one devoted and docile mare who was my younger sister's mount, who came out of her stall one evening unable to walk on one front foot. We couldn't determine what the trouble was and immediately called the vet, who, being busy taking care of handsome show horses, wasn't able to come immediately. We were distressed, and when he did arrive, rushed him down to the barn to look at our pet. When he asked us how old she was we couldn't answer. He looked in her mouth. "My word," he drawled, "this mare must've voted for McKinley!" But he looked at her leg anyway and found she had a cocked ankle — she had twisted it somehow. He jerked it about and prescribed ice packs all night long. We all scurried to the kitchen, pulled out the ice trays, which meant no cold drinks for us on that hot night, and busily started crushing ice, a luxury we seldom afforded even guests. My sister tore a pair of blue jeans in half, sewed up the bottom of the leg and arranged a sling effect to go over the mare's shoulder. We slipped the pants leg over her foot, filled it with our precious crushed ice and tied the sling about her shoulder, and tightened the cloth around her leg. The expression on her little black face clearly showed that she was bewildered by and unaccustomed to this extreme care, which she had never known in *all* her years. But she and we persevered throughout the night, and while we became the laughingstock of the county, the mare was cured and all lived happily ever after. What fools even the sternest of men become when involved with a horse!

Your horse must be kept well shod. Remember the old saying, "For want of a nail a shoe was lost, for want of a shoe a foot was lost, for want of a foot a horse was lost, and for want of a horse, a rider was lost!" Your horse should have new shoes once a month, for a poorly shod horse becomes unsafe and often lame. A hunter's feet should never become too long because it will cause him to stumble, and it is particularly bad when landing after a jump. If he is to be worked in the winter on snow and ice, he should have special snowshoes so he won't slip. If you are lucky enough to have a good blacksmith, respect his opinions thoroughly, for much depends on the shoe of a horse. If your horse is going lame, tell your blacksmith about it, for he may be able to suggest a helpful type of shoe. Often high-heeled shoes, heel-bar, center-bar, or padded shoes, can correct lameness entirely, depending on its nature. And if your blacksmith is likely not to be able to come at your beck and call, it is a good idea to have a pair of pincers handy should a shoe come loose, so you can pull it off yourself. You might also have a rasp and a paring knife about so you can keep the bare foot trimmed until the blacksmith's next visit.

As far as clothes are concerned, your horse should have a complete wardrobe of pajamas, robes, and a nightcap. That is, for cool nights he should have a lightweight sheet, when the frost comes, he should have two heavy blankets, and for cooling him out after a workout, he should have a lightweight cooler of wool. Each horse should have his own leather halter.

During cold weather, any horse who is in work and has grown a heavy coat should be clipped to prevent his catching cold. Hunters should be given the hunter clip, that is, leaving the thick coat under the saddle and on his legs up to the elbow in front and the stifle behind, to protect his legs, especially if he is actually being hunted, and to protect his back from the saddle. A saddle horse is clipped all over. Most thoroughbred horses never grow too thick a coat, and if a sheet is kept on them from the beginning of the cool nights their coats will stay down and they will remain sleek and shiny all winter long.

WINNING YOUR SPURS

Above all, take good care of your horse and pamper him a little — he deserves it. *Never* punish him with neglect. A happy horse is a happy ride.

SUMMARY

Every rider should know how to tack and untack, groom and feed his horse. He must learn about bits, of which there are three basic types: snaffle, Pelham, and double. There are three kinds of martingales: standing, running and Irish. There are two basic types of saddles: flat and forward-seat, for jumping. A horse should be thoroughly groomed every day with currycomb, stiff brush, body brush and rub-rag. His feet should be cleaned with a hoof pick to prevent thrush. The feeding schedule and the amounts and types of feed vary with individual horses according to their condition and the amount of work they are doing. Feed should include grain, bran, hay and plenty of water. A horse should be well shod at all times, and special shoes can often correct lameness. Every horse should have a sheet, blankets, a cooler and a halter. Simple medicines and leg bandages should always be kept on hand. In short, you should take the best possible care of your horse at all times and never neglect him.

PART TWO

Showmanship

THE AIKEN
A common hunter jump of brush and rails.

THE BRUSH
A common hunter jump.

76

CHAPTER X

The Horse Show

A HORSE SHOW IS FUN. Don't ever think of it as anything *but* fun. You're there to show how well your horse can perform, to measure his ability and yours against friendly competition. It's nothing more than a big game, and should be entered into as such. Granted, in the bigger shows competition is keen enough to make it more serious, but nonetheless, you're out to do your very best regardless of the competition. Win or lose, you should be able to come home from a show with the feeling that you and your horse did a good job. In certain quarters, the show game has turned into a game of high stakes, where the challenge is not who can do the best, but who has enough money to buy the best horse and the best rider. This makes it even more important for you, as an individual, through your own attitude, to keep showing as close as possible to the friendly gathering of neighbors curious to see whose horse can perform the best, which is what showing was originally intended to be.

Sportsmanship is your keynote, and no matter how bitter your disappointments in showing, never forget how to smile and mean it. Without sportsmanship, showing becomes a cutthroat business, competitors become enemies, and judges become ogres. The horse-show world is very small, so your role as an individual is important, and it is your responsibility to keep the true spirit of sportsmanlike competition alive.

When you are riding in the show ring or over an outside course you should have nothing on your mind but your horse and your performance. Forget that anyone else is around and just remember how to ride. You're not riding to beat the others in the class, you're riding to make a good showing. If you win, and you know you had a good performance, fine. If you win, though you had a poor performance, realize that you were just lucky that no one else had a good performance either, don't pat yourself on the back. If you had a good performance and didn't win, it doesn't mean that you were robbed or that the judge was prejudiced, it only means that your best was not as good as someone else's. You don't gripe or complain, you just try harder the next time. For all the ribbons you think you should have won, there are twice as many you have won or will win without deserving them.

As far as the judges are concerned, remember that they are out there to do their very best. It's not easy to decide on four winners out of a field of forty, and sometimes the performances are all so bad that it's a matter of deciding which were the *least* bad! A judge can't see every horse every second, but he can see a great deal more from the center of the ring than you can from the outside or from the top of your own horse. Furthermore, they know a lot better what they are looking for than you do, so have some respect for their opinions. The only time it even comes down to a matter of their personal preferences is in a case where two riders or horses seem to be absolutely equal in performance, which is seldom. And, incidentally, judges are not infallible, so don't condemn them for an occasional mistake, though it may have meant a lot to you. They *are* human.

Almost all shows are recognized members of the American Horse Shows Association and are governed by its rules. Recognized shows include Regular Show Members (shows elected to membership with the Association), Local Show Members (shows which are limited in duration, number of classes, and total cash prizes), Licensed Shows (shows which are licensed for one year only), and Honorary Show Members (certain foreign shows including the International Horse Show of London, the Dublin Horse Show and others).

Points won at any Recognized Show, except Local Show Members, are counted in computing the annual Division High Score Awards made by the Association. The number of points awarded for each ribbon varies according to the classification of the show under the system set up by the Association to equalize competition for the High Score Awards. Class A shows count triple points, Class B shows double, Class C shows are counted normally. A show may choose its own classification or classifications. It may be A in one division, B in another and C in another. For example, it may be A in green conformation and green working hunters, B in regular conformation and regular working, and C in jumpers. Divisions are rated according to the following specifications:

CLASS A: Regular Conformation, 8 classes and a minimum of $1000 in cash premiums; Green Conformation, 6 classes and $600; Regular Working, 7 classes and $700; Green Working, 6 classes and $500; Pony, 9 classes and $500; Jumpers, 7 classes and $1000; Harness Ponies, 7 classes and $1000; Harness Show Ponies, 6 classes and $750; 3-Gaited Saddle Horses, 8 classes and $2000; 5-Gaited, 7 classes and $2000; Fine Harness, 5 classes and $1250; Parade Horses, 4 classes and $750; Roadsters, 5 classes and $1250; Walking Horses, 5 classes and $1250; Arabians, 7 classes and $500; Morgans, 5 classes and $300.

CLASS B: Regular Conformation, 6 classes and $500; Green Conformation, 4

THE HOG BACK
An open-jumper fence. This usually has a brush underneath the middle rail.

classes and $300; Regular Working, 4 classes and $300; Green Working, 4 classes and $250; Pony, 5 classes and $200; Jumpers, 5 classes and $500; Harness Ponies, 4 classes and $500; Harness Show Ponies, 4 classes and $400; 3-Gaited, 4 classes and $600; 5-Gaited, 4 classes and $600; Fine Harness, 3 classes and $400; Parade Horses, 3 classes and $400; Roadsters, 3 classes and $450; Walking Horses, 3 classes and $450; Arabians, 4 classes and $200; Morgans, 3 classes and $150.

Generally speaking, breeding, team, pair, warm-up, championship preliminary and final, local, children's, bareback, grooms', and costume classes do not count in the rating of a division. In pony sections classes open to both ponies and horses do not count, and in horse sections, pony classes do not count. It is perfectly possible for a show to qualify for an A or B rating "across the board," when all its divisions meet the requirements of that particular classification.

Everyone who shows or plans to show should be a member of the AHSA and keep his rule book handy whenever showing. It is not only an advantage but a necessity. The following class and division requirement explanations are based on the rule book definitions:

A *Maiden* is a horse or a rider who has not won one first ribbon at a Recognized Show (except Local Show Members) in the division in which he is showing. That is, a champion open jumper can be a maiden hunter, although Equitation is considered as a single division, whether Saddle Horse Seat or Hunting Seat. Winnings within a division shall not count in reckoning a horse's status in another classification (such as 3-gaited to 5-gaited) except in the Hunter Division, where winnings in one section count in another section.

A *Novice* is the same as above, the limitation being three firsts.

A *Limit* is the same as above, the limitation being six firsts.

An *Open* class is open to all horses or riders, regardless of age or winnings. An open horsemanship class, however, generally specifies an age limit.

The maximum age limitation in Maiden, Novice and Limit classes is generally seventeen (*i.e.* not having reached the eighteenth birthday). The maximum age allowed in other horsemanship classes varies considerably, and there is agitation at present to standardize the maximum age at seventeen, eighteen, or nineteen years.

A *Local* class is one for which an entry must reside within a specified territory.

An *Amateur* class is open only to contestants who are bona fide amateurs and, as such, must possess an Amateur Card of the AHSA or sign the Amateur Affidavit Form available at the show. An amateur, briefly, is one who does not earn his livelihood through horses or accept any remuneration for his activities in that field, with the exception of judging. For this reason, the awarding of money prizes in equitation classes is strictly forbidden, as the acceptance thereof would make the recipient a professional.

EQUITATION DIVISION

This division has been divided into three distinct sections, saddle horses, hunting and stock-saddle seats, though first ribbons won in any one section are counted in the reckoning of Maiden, Novice or Limit status. Ribbons won in classes where the contestants are not required to ride at all gaits are not counted in this reckoning.

Fall of horse or rider eliminates the rider, and any rider who does not have his horse under sufficient control may be dismissed from the ring by the judge.

Saddle Horse Seat

Martingales and spurs are prohibited, while crops are optional.

The general requirements for these classes are as follows, though they will vary according to the particular class and the judge's wishes:

Walk, trot and canter in both directions, reversing *either* toward or away from the rail.

Dismounting and mounting, without aid; backing (always back at least three full steps); individual performance at the rail or around the ring; figure eight at trot and canter.

For your individual performance at the rail or around the ring you may be asked something like this: trot down one side, changing diagonals in the middle, stop, reverse, canter on the correct lead stopping at the middle and changing to the false lead, and stop at the judge's command. When you are asked for an individual performance, every step must be calculated two strides ahead, and it must be perfect. Be perfectly calm and keep your horse collected so he will obey your commands immediately. When you trot, make it a strong full trot, and change exactly in the middle if you have been asked to do so. When you canter, canter slowly, preparing to stop your horse and change leads *before* you come to the appointed place for the change. Watch where you are going and look ahead so that you can prepare for your next move. When you stop, stop completely and stand still. If you are to stop at the judge's command, be ready before he gives it so that you can stop immediately. If you get on the wrong lead when cantering, stop immediately and change it. You'll get far more credit for trying even if you don't succeed, than for going along on the wrong lead as if you didn't know the difference.

THE STONE WALL
A common jump for hunters or jumpers. This is usually made of stone with a rail over it on an outside course, or of painted wood, often with loose blocks on the top.

For your figure eight *always* face the rail — this is half your battle. If you have been asked to trot up the side of the ring before the figure eight, don't cut for your eight in the center of the end, go all the way around the end and then turn so you will be facing the rail and make that the first circle of your eight. Be sure to change diagonal precisely in the center of the eight, not before, not after, but precisely in the center. After you have made one circle in each direction at a trot, stop your horse perfectly straight, facing the rail, collecting your horse completely and, *without leaning over,* ask him to canter with the correct aids. If he takes the wrong lead, stop and try again. Make a complete circle, stopping again in the center of the eight, and canter on the other lead, being sure to complete the circle right to the center of the eight. Then stop completely, and back three full steps. Then walk forward a step or two and walk back to the line of horses. Be sure to make an even eight, not with one circle larger than the other, and try to make both circles as small as possible. The important thing to remember in the figure eight is to look two strides ahead all the time. Start turning before you think you have to, and look immediately toward the very center of the eight. If you don't watch where you're going, the horse's momentum, especially at the canter, will carry you across the ring before you have time to turn him.

If you should be asked to canter down the center of the ring, changing leads every third stride, don't gasp and throw your hands up — it's not so difficult. The secret is in keeping your horse very slow and well collected, and count the strides as you go. As you count the second stride, immediately stop him, for he will have time for one more stride before he stops completely, and *without turning his head or body,* give the signal for the opposite lead. Be sure to stop him completely, there should be no step in between the two leads, certainly not a step of a trot. If he should start to trot, bring him back immediately and insist on the lead you want.

Individual performances and figure eights should be done perfectly smoothly, and the hands should never move an inch from their correct position. It's all done with those two little fingers, closing them on one hand for a turn, and closing both hands for a stop. And when asking for your canter, don't lean forward or bend over — it throws your horse off balance and off stride and makes it more difficult for you to make him canter.

You may be asked to change horses with someone else in the class. In this case, you dismount, slip your stirrups off the saddle, being careful to keep the left one on the left side and the right on the right side, and put them on the other horse's saddle. Your performance on your competitor's horse will depend very much upon how alert you have been during the class, and whether or not you have been watching all the other individual performances. If you have watched attentively, you will know which horse has a bad mouth, which one has a light one, which horse is easy to put into a canter, and which horse is difficult. You will know if a certain horse wouldn't take one lead or the other, or if one was hard to back. Knowing these things, you will know before you get on the strange horse what things you will have to watch, what things you will have to concentrate on. If you're lucky, your instructor will come into the ring to help you change horses, and he will tell you what to be careful of on this

THE DOUBLE OXER

An open-jump fence. The single oxer does not have the first rail.

particular horse. Whenever you are in or out of the ring during a horsemanship class, watch every horse, for you may be put up on him at any minute.

You may aso be asked to ride a perfectly strange horse which is supplied by the committee, though this seldom happens. If you are, be cautious as you ride him and feel him out till you know how he responds to the aids.

You may be asked to ride without stirrups, which is something anyone should be able to do. In this case, ride just as if you had stirrups, perhaps increasing the grip of your upper leg so that you will remain perfectly still and secure in the saddle.

Hunting Seat

Martingales and spurs (unroweled) are permissible in hunting-seat classes, but should not be used unless absolutely necessary.

Entrants may be asked to walk, trot and canter, or to jump, according to the specifications of the class as stated in the prize list and show catalogue.

General requirements, which vary with the particular classes, are as follows: walk, trot, and canter; back; gallop and stop; pull up on turns between fences; jump fence in middle of ring in line with course or at right angles to course; jump low fences at walk and trot as well as canter; change horses; jump strange horse supplied by committee; figure eight at trot, changing diagonals; figure eight at canter with flying or stationary change of lead; ride without stirrups.

If you are asked to gallop and stop, you will probably have to stop at the judge's command, which means you will have to be *ready* to stop at any instant. If you are lucky enough to have an appointed place at which to stop, you can keep your eye on the spot and, keeping your pace up, prepare to stop two or three strides before you reach it. You must *not* slacken your pace as you approach the appointed place. If you *are* asked to gallop, it means gallop, and not just a fast canter or hand gallop. You should come down the ring at full speed, in galloping position, and pull up quickly. The pulley rein is an excellent aid for this purpose, but it must not be rough. When you have stopped, you should back three steps, go forward and walk back to the line.

The pulley rein should also be used for stopping on a turn between fences, bringing your horse to a halt, and starting out again slowly.

If you should be asked to canter over one fence, pull up and trot over the next, be sure you stop completely before going forward again, and as you do go forward, keep your horse thoroughly collected in a slow trot. After you have stopped you must be careful to give your horse just enough rein so that he won't misunderstand you and break into a canter again, but you must not give him so much that he lunges forward at top speed either. It's very important to hold him in until the very last second before he takes off, for you must trot over the fence, and this excludes even a single stride of canter. If he breaks before you reach the fence, bring him back to a trot again and insist on his keeping that gait.

When required to jump a fence in the middle of the ring either in line with or at right angles to the course, the important thing is keeping your eyes up and watching where you are going. As you jump the fence before you have to turn you must actually be looking at the fence in the middle of the ring. If it is a very sharp turn, you will actually have to start your turn while you are still in mid-air, jumping the fence at something of an angle. If you look at the fence in the middle and ride right toward it you will have no trouble. Then, as you jump the fence in the middle of the ring, you must again start looking for your next fence, which is on the side of the ring, and prepare to turn toward it. If you are just a second late with the turn you will either be off course or make an awfully rough turn.

Your figure eight in hunting-seat classes is just as important as in saddle-seat classes. You should do it just the same way, being just as careful about changing diagonals and leads, and being sure to face the rail. If you are asked for a flying change of lead at the figure eight it means that you are to change leads without stopping. If you have a horse you know you can depend upon for a flying change, you need only change his direction abruptly enough to make change leads, but don't depend upon it unless you have schooled him for it. If you are on a horse you are not sure will do a flying lead change by himself, you must bring him back so that he is going slowly enough to obey your command for a change of lead, but he must not break into a trot.

84

The shifting of the rider's weight from the one side to the other is very important in the flying change, and with a horse schooled to do a flying change the shifting of your weight alone may change him.

Shows offering full divisions for both saddle seat and hunting seat usually offer a championship and reserve for each division. As a rule, first and second ribbon winners in each class qualify for the championship class in their division. If there is only one championship for both hunting seat and saddle seat, first and second ribbon winners in all equitation classes shall be eligible.

AHSA Medal classes are now offered in all three sections of the Equitation Division — Saddle Horse Seat, Hunting Seat and Stock Saddle Seat. To be eligible, a rider must not have reached his or her eighteenth birthday and must be a Junior Member of the Association. For AHSA. Zones 1 and 2, three blues are required for eligibility in the finals, which are held at a Recognized Show in the Eastern United States. For Zones 3 through 7, only one blue is required for eligibility. The finals for stock-saddle seat are held at a Pacific Coast show, and only one blue is required for eligibility.

The most coveted saddle-horse seat award is undoubtedly the NHSA Good Hands Trophy, which is awarded at the National Horse Show at Madison Square Garden. This is for children who have not reached their seventeenth birthday, and to become eligible for this class at the Garden a rider must win the Good Hands class at a recognized horse show, after which he is eliminated from further competition for the remainder of the year until after the final competition at the Garden. After winning this class at the Garden a rider is eliminated from any further competition in Good Hands classes.

Similar to the Good Hands is the ASPCA Alfred B. Maclay Trophy, which is considered the highest award for hunting-seat equitation. A rider is eligible for this class at the Garden after having won the Maclay at a Recognized Show, and is ineligible

THE IN-AND-OUT
Found on nearly every hunter course, this is usually enclosed, with the fences about twenty-four feet apart.

for further competition in this class until after the Garden. The winner at the Garden is eliminated from any further competition in the Maclay. This is also open only to children who have not reached their seventeenth birthday. If the final competition for either of these trophies falls after the date of the child's seventeenth birthday, he is still eligible to ride in the final competition if he has won a Maclay class prior to his birthday.

The Maclay and Good Hands Trophies are the most prized awards in horsemanship, and on a few occasions, the same rider has won both trophies the same year. Unwritten law proclaims that the winner of either of these trophies at the Garden is to retire from horsemanship in that division, in the tradition of true sportsmanship.

HUNTER DIVISION

A hunter course shall be at least four feet high, but not exceed four feet six inches, and is to simulate fences found in the hunt field, that is, brush, aiken, stone wall, white board gate or fence, chicken coop, post and rail, etc. All fences should have wings or be of sufficient width to simulate natural obstacles. There should be at least eight fences, and the performance starts when the horse starts over the course and ends about fifty feet beyond the last fence. Horses must be over 14.2 hands, except in pony or junior classes. Where there are both conformation and working-hunter sections, green or regular, one horse may not compete in both sections.

"Small" hunters must not exceed 15.2½ hands, "Lightweight" must be up to carrying 165 pounds, "Middleweight" up to carrying 185 pounds, and "Heavyweight" up to carrying 205 pounds. Thoroughbreds must be registered in the American stud book, non-thoroughbreds must not be registered.

Regular conformation or working hunters are horses who are shown over regular hunter courses. A green hunter, conformation or working, must not have been shown at a Recognized Show prior to January first of the current year, except prior to January first of his four-year-old year. A horse's age is always figured from January first of the year he is foaled. A Qualified hunter must have a certificate from the M.F.H. of a recognized or registered pack of hounds that the horse has hunted satisfactorily for one or more seasons with the pack. Such a certificate is only valid for two years after the last season he was hunted, after which he must be requalified.

Championships in hunter divisions are awarded on points won as specified in the rule book. At A and B shows a championship preliminary is held for each division, to be judged under saddle, and all horses eligible must compete unless excused by a veterinary due to unsoundness, or by the committee, or forfeit all points won. Martingales are prohibited in championship preliminaries.

86

SHOWMANSHIP

In conformation classes, performance counts either 75 per cent or 60 per cent, conformation either 25 per cent or 40 per cent, according to show specifications. In working classes, performance and way of going count 100 per cent. Horses must be "serviceably sound" for all hunter classes, and any signs of lameness, broken wind or impaired vision will disqualify a horse for an award. This rule does not apply to

THE SINGLE RAIL
An open-jumper fence to which all hunters should also be accustomed.

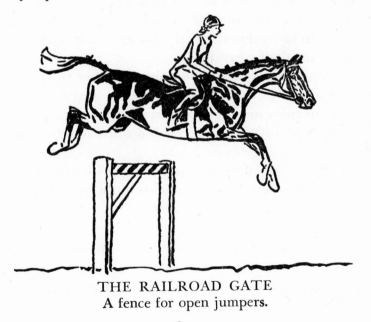

THE RAILROAD GATE
A fence for open jumpers.

breeding classes. Types of hunter classes vary with each show and their specifications are printed in the prize list and in the show catalogue.

JUMPER DIVISION

Jumpers may be of any height — except in pony classes — any description, and any degree of soundness. In jumper classes the course starts as soon as the horse enters the ring and ends approximately twenty-four feet after the last jump. One circle, at any gait, upon entering the ring, is allowed. Any additional circles will be counted as disobediences. From the first jump to the last the horse must maintain a trot, canter or gallop under penalty of a disobedience, except in the case of a refusal or runout. Fences may be of any height and type, according to the specifications of the individual show, but all courses must be illustrated or clearly described in the prize list. However, a single-rail jump may not be raised higher than four and one half feet, and double crossed rails are not to be used. All brush fences must have a clearly visible rail placed on, above or beyond the fence. The courses in Class A shows must meet certain specifications as explained in the rule book, and effective January 1, 1955, these specifications shall be mandatory for Class B shows as well.

Shows may now include a Green Jumper Section in their Jumper Division. This section is open to horses who have not won twelve blues in Recognized Shows as of the opening of the show in question, and effective January 1, 1955, will be restricted to horses who have not been shown in the Jumper Division of a Recognized Show prior to January first of the current year and who have not subsequently won twelve blues in the Jumper Division. Fences in the Green Jumper Section may not exceed three feet nine inches for the first round.

Due to the increasing interest in Olympic and other international competition, most shows now include at least one Olympic class judged under FEI (International Equestrian Federation) rules in order to train both riders and horses for such competition. Such a class is required of Class A shows and, effective January 1, 1955, of Class B shows.

Below are described some of the *major* differences between AHSA jumper rules and FEI rules, though both are too lengthy and complicated to cover in full.

	AHSA	FEI
Touches:	Front, 1 fault; hind, ½ fault.	Not counted.
Knockdowns:	Front, 4 faults; hind, 2 faults.	Either — 4 faults.
Fall of horse or rider:	Elimination.	Eight faults.

SHOWMANSHIP

	AHSA	FEI
Time limit:	None, except in Scurry or Handy classes.	Based on minimum speed of 380 yds. per minute. Penalty or elimination. (In Olympic Games the minimum speed is 436 yds. per minute.)
Rider's weight:	None specified.	Minimum of 165 lbs. for males, 154 lbs. for females.
Disobediences: (runout, refusal, circle or deviations, loss of gait or resistance)	Three faults for first, six for second, and elimination for three. Cumulative for whole round.	Same as AHSA, but resistance or loss of gait for 60 seconds is penalized by elimination.
Riding off course:	Elimination.	Elimination.
Showing obstacle to horse:	Disobedience.	Elimination.
Double, treble and multiple jumps, enclosed in-and-outs: (maximum distance of 39 ft. between elements)	In the case of disobedience at one element of double or treble jump, horse must rejump previous elements; in case of multiple jumps, the horse retakes course where disobedience occurred. On *enclosed* in-and-outs, only the one element at which disobedience occurred need be rejumped, but this must be done within 60 seconds under penalty of elimination.	In case of disobedience or fall at one element of double, treble or multiple jump, all elements must be rejumped or horse is eliminated. Faults are scored on each element and totaled. On *enclosed* in-and-outs, only the one element at which disobedience or fall occurred need be rejumped.
Fault-and-out class:	Known as "touch-and-out," as touches count, as well as any comparable fault. In "knockdown-and-out" touches are not counted. In the case of a fall, the horse is credited with obstacles already cleared.	Round is finished after first fault, be it a fall, disobedience, knockdown or time penalty. If it occurred at a fence, horse must jump the next obstacle. Time and number of obstacles cleared without fault determine winner.
Jump-offs:	Course may be shortened by not more than 50 per cent. If horses tied had clean rounds, jumps are raised and broadened. All ties involving first place must be jumped off. A fall eliminates horse from further competition, but not from award already earned before jump-off.	Since time is counted and an excess of the time limit penalized ¼ fault per second, there is seldom need for a jump-off, except in the case of fault-and-out, where a certain number of obstacles may have been cleared by two competitors in the same time. When necessary a shortened course may be used and time counted.
Faults counted:	From entry into ring until crossing of finish line.	Between the starting and finishing lines.

89

WINNING YOUR SPURS

SUMMARY

Showing should be entered into for the sport alone. It's a big game, and as such certain rules and regulations are necessary, and you, as an exhibitor or rider must know the rules and abide by them. Shows vary in importance and in classification by the AHSA: Regular Show Members, Local Show Members, Licensed Show Members, and Honorary Show Members; these are classified as A, B, or C shows according to numbers of classes and amounts of cash premiums. Shows offer any or all of several divisions including Hunters — Conformation, Green, Working; Horsemanship — Hunting Seat, Saddle Seat, Stock Saddle Seat; Open Jumpers — under AHSA and FEI rules; Saddle Horses — 3-Gaited and 5-Gaited; and others. You must be sure to know the specifications of each class you enter and be ready to execute them. Your whole aim, however, is to be a good sportsman and a good competitor.

CHAPTER XI

Preparing for the Show

NOW THAT YOU have carefully made out your entries from the prize list, it's time it's time to start preparing for the show. There's much to be done, so don't waste any time.

The first thing you must do is to set up in your own ring the courses which you and your horse will be jumping in the show. The longer the time you have to school over the courses, the better. If you're entering the hunting-seat Medal class and the Maclay, set up each of those courses and school over them until you and your horse are able to perform smoothly over them. The Medal course simulates a figure eight, so you must concentrate on looking for the next fence and riding toward each fence directly from the fence before it so that your turns will be smooth. You have to school your horse so that he won't try to run out on the fences in the middle of the ring. If he should run out to the right, for example, be sure to pull the left rein immediately, don't let him complete the circle toward the right. If he runs out to the left, pull the right rein. If you let him get away with it entirely without pulling him back on course, he will be that much harder to keep in line the next time, and that much harder to school. As you approach the fence the next time, keep more pressure on the rein on the side opposite that toward which he ran out and catch him before he tries it again.

If you have entered your horse in hunter classes, set up a brush fence, a white gate, a post and rail and a stone wall or chicken coop and school your horse over this course, twice around until he is used to it and jumps every fence right. If there's going to be an in-and-out at the show, school him over that too. For this, the two post and rail fences should be twenty-four feet apart, and if he quits at the second fence, back him up and make him jump it from where he would land from the first fence, don't take him back and let him jump the whole in-and-out again. And be sure all the fences are the same height as the fences will be at the show, or even a few inches higher.

If you are going to be in a hunter hack class, you should school your horse to walk, trot and canter on a loose rein. The best way to do this is to trot him on a very loose rein, letting him trot as fast as he wants until he breaks into a canter, and when he does break, punish him by bringing him back to a trot immediately. He'll learn that he should trot fast but not break into a canter. Then teach him to canter very slowly on a long rein, and any time he starts going too fast, bring him right back to the speed you want. You should use your voice a lot when schooling him for a loose rein so that when you're in the ring he will slow down at the sound of your voice. Then set up two three-foot six-inch fences on one side of the ring, canter him slowly over them, on a loose rein, gallop up the other side of the ring and stop him short and back, for this is what you will have to do in the show.

If you are going into horsemanship classes, be sure to practice your figure eights until they are perfect and your horse knows what they are all about. If necessary, canter him around and around in one half of it until he has learned how to make the circles perfectly round. If your horse has no idea of how to do a figure eight, first work him in circles, at the trot and then the canter, making the circles smaller and smaller each time until he has learned how to keep his gait in a very small circle. Then put the two circles together and you have a figure eight. While you're schooling, don't let him know that you are only making one circle in each direction before

MOUNTING AND DISMOUNTING

1. Facing the rear of the horse, pick up the reins with your left hand and turn the stirrup toward you with your right hand. Standing on your right toe, place your left foot in the stirrup, toe down.

2. Place your right hand on the cantle of the saddle and, jumping off your right foot, balance yourself against the horse. If necessary, reach over the seat of the saddle and hold the far side to help pull yourself into position.

3. Swing your right leg high over the horse's rump, moving your right hand forward to the pommel of the saddle. Pick up the right stirrup by turning your right toe inward, and settle your weight down into the saddle slowly.

To dismount: Take the reins in your left hand and drop the right stirrup. Put your weight in the left stirrup and swing your right foot up and over the horse's rump, placing your right hand on the cantle of the saddle. Balancing your weight on your hands, drop the left stirrup and slide down to the ground, moving immediately to the front of the horse.

stopping to change leads at the canter, for he will learn to break from the canter into a trot before you have reached the center of the figure eight. Also practice rail performance, changing leads several times during the length of the ring, cantering, stopping and backing, galloping and stopping short, and so forth. At least half your performance in the show ring depends on how much you have schooled yourself and your horse.

If you have entered your horse in open jumper classes, set up the exact courses, just as they are outlined in the prize list, and school over them, without wings. School over high fences so that you will be prepared if you are in a jump-off over higher fences. Furthermore, if you school over good big fences, your horse will hit them a couple of times and sting his legs so that he'll have real respect for those bars. School over broad jumps, such as hog's backs, triple bars and liverpools, over single rails, preferably striped, railroad gates, and all the funniest-looking fences you can build so that you will be ready for whatever they put up in the show ring.

If you are in a handy hunter class, practice jumping fences at angles, making sharp turns, and leading your horse over a fence. Often in these classes the rider is to ride his horse up to one fence, push off the top bar, back up, dismount, and lead the horse over the fence. If you practice dropping the top rail you will learn how to do it so that it drops right next to the fence rather than two or three feet away, making the jump that much broader for your horse. And you had better school yourself at jumping over the fence as you lead your horse over. One time I, who fancied myself to be athletic, suffered great embarrassment at a major show when I was unable to get my own feet over a two foot fence without knocking it down. I must have tried it ten times before I made it, and my horse won the class, probably more by virtue of his patience than his performance!

For any kind of hack class you will probably have to dismount and mount while your horse stands perfectly still, so you had better practice this, too, punishing your horse if he moves. Practice it many times, so that he will be used to your hopping off and on him. And as you mount, try not to crawl all over his back. Don't scrape your foot across his rump or land heavily in your saddle, for you can hardly blame your horse for objecting to this sort of nonsense.

Don't forget that if you are in any conformation hunter classes you will have to line your horse up so that he is standing on all fours and looks his best. Practice this with a whip in your hand. His two front feet should be straight under him and in line with one another, while one hind foot should be slightly in front of the other. Some horses, happily, are co-operative enough to stop naturally in this position, but the majority are not. First walk your horse forward and stop him. If his feet are not right, back him step by step until they are. If you pull him forward, he will most likely move only his front feet and end up stretching like a saddle horse. On the other hand, when you back him, be careful he does not end up with all feet under him like a trained seal standing on a ball. There is nothing worse-looking than a horse standing with both hind feet under his stomach. Once you have finally got him in the right stance by backing and moving a step forward if one front foot is behind the other, keep him there. Take your reins by the buckles and stand way out in front of him, keeping his head up and keeping him still by jiggling the reins a little as you stand.

SHOWMANSHIP

Don't stand close to him, you should be about two feet in front of him so that he can be clearly seen by the judge and so that he will stretch his head and neck out. As the judge looks at him in the show, get his attention by waving something at him, such as grass. This will make him stretch his nose out so he will look good. As you school him to stand in this same position for as long as ten minutes, if he starts creeping up on you, jerk the reins hard and slap him lightly on the chest with your crop. He mustn't get the idea he can climb all over you. He must keep his distance, stand still, and look alert.

The day before the show you must get your horse all trimmed up. Clip the whiskers on his chin and muzzle, the long hairs around his eyes, the insides of his ears, and, if he needs it, his fetlocks. Cold-blooded, or common-bred horses often grow longish, thick hair on the back and bottom of the fetlock. Thoroughbreds seldom do. Comb and thin the mane and tail, and groom him thoroughly.

Just before he is to be vanned, wrap each leg up in sheet cotton and shipping bandages to protect them in shipping. Put a tail guard or a wet bandage on his tail to protect it from rubbing against the back of the van. According to the weather, put a sheet or blanket on him. If he is being shipped in a fairly open van be sure to put a sheet on him to protect him from drafts, for a horse often gets overheated from nervousness when being shipped and a draft can give him a cold. His halter should have a sheepskin lining on the noseband, or at least a cotton bandage wrapped around it so that it won't rub his nose raw as he moves about in the van.

With each horse you should send two pails, one for water and one for feed, and two shanks, either rope or leather. Also send along enough grain, bran and hay for the duration of the show. Straw is usually available at shows, as is feed, but it is far better to bring your own feed along since that is what your horse is used to. You should have some kind of tack trunk, and this and your pails should be painted with your stable colors and name or initials. In the bottom of your tack trunk you should put your saddle, with an extra stirrup leather and an extra stirrup also, if you have one, for either leather or iron may break during the show and you will be out of luck without an extra. You should send as many bridles as necessary, but if you only need one, it is well to take an extra along in case anything gets broken. It's awfully easy for a horse to step on a rein or get the bridle caught up in his stall and break it. In short, take all the tack you need, making allowance for breakage.

Be sure to take all your grooming equipment and a big-eyed needle and strong wool the color of your horse's mane for braiding. Take any medicine you use regularly plus liniment, white lotion, bluing, vaseline and colic tonic. Take an extra supply of sheet cotton and cotton bandages for wrapping up his legs at night. Be prepared for almost anything, for horses have a wonderful capacity for getting sick or wounded during shows. In warm weather be sure to take salt along, and also your sponge, pail

95

and scraper. These are not usually necessary during cold weather, but might come in handy even then if you have room for them.

Once you have packed your horse and all his belongings on the van, you can go home and start worrying about what *you* are going to wear. If you are going into hunter classes, you will need some formal attire as well as ratcatcher, or casual. Below is a checklist for your suitcase.

	FORMAL	RATCATCHER
Boots	Plain black; patent tops with tabs *not* sewn down optional	Black, brown, or jodhpur boots and leggings
Breeches	Canary-yellow or buff twill or cord, button leg	Any color
Shirt	White stock shirt, French cuffs with cuff links	Any color or style
Vest	Canary-yellow, gold buttons	Any color, buttons optional
Coat	Black melton or oxford-gray, or cutaway (weasel belly), or swallow-tail (shad belly)	Any color or material
Hat	Black derby with guard; hunt cap optional except in appointments classes	Derby or hunt cap
Gloves	Pigskin; also white string	Any or none
Stock	Plain white, not ready-tied, with horizontal gold safety pin	Any color or none, scarf or tie
Whips	Hunt whip; feathered bat	Any; feathered bat preferable
Spurs	Small hunting spurs, no rowels	Any, without rowels

For appointments classes, such as hunt teams or corinthian classes, personal attire is very important and must adhere strictly to the rule book. The above formal attire is correct for a lady member riding astride, but if weasel-belly or shad-belly coat is worn a high silk hat is required.

A stock which is bought ready-tied and is made in two pieces is absolutely not acceptable in appointments classes, and should never be worn. The reason for wearing a real stock out hunting is that in the case of an accident this length of material can be used as a sling for a broken arm or a tourniquet to stop bleeding. This is also the reason that a plain-gold safety pin must be used to hold the stock in position, and the safety pin must always be pinned horizontally, never vertically, for in the case of an accident a vertical pin could easily impale you. If you cannot tie your own stock properly, ask someone to do it for you. There is nothing worse than a misshapen or weary-looking stock.

To tie your stock properly, first hold the entire length of material in front of you with both hands, placing it against your neck at a point about two inches off the center of the stock, buttoning the stock onto your shirt. If the stock has no buttonhole, a small pin may be used. With the ends of the stock again held in each hand, cross the ends behind your head, running one end through the slit in the other. If there is no slit provided, simply smooth down the point at which the ends cross. Bring the ends to the front again and tie a square knot. This is done by crossing the long end, let's say it's the right end in this case, over the other end, bringing it up through the loop in half a knot. Then this right end will hang straight down over the other. Holding the underneath end, formerly the left end, with your left hand, cross the top end over it once more, bringing it up through the new loop. Pull the top end to the right, and the bottom end to the left so that your knot is perfectly square. Smoothing out the wrinkles of the knot, draw the right end upwards and fold it over the knot, preferably pinning it against the collar of your shirt underneath the fold so that it will stay high under your chin. Then do the same thing with the left end, bringing it as high as possible and securing it with a small concealed safety pin. Where the two ends cross over the knot, insert your gold safety pin, catching part of the knot as well as the two ends, helping to keep the stock in place. The bottoms of the two ends of the stock should be pinned at either side of your shirt underneath your vest so that they will not straighten out and pull at the knot.

Also in appointments classes you must carry a hunting whip. Gentlemen members carry this whip with the thong hanging, not looped, while lady members are permitted to loop the thong, lash end toward the handle, and a part of the thong will hang down the horse's shoulder. The hunting whip is not held at the end, near the handle, but a third of the way away from the handle, two thirds of the distance from the thong end. You may be required to crack your whip in hunt-team classes.

For appointments classes your horse must have special equipment, too. The bridle may be double, Pelham or snaffle, but reins must be sewn onto bit. It is no longer required that cheekpieces also be sewn onto bit. Rubber-covered reins are not permissible, and a cavesson noseband must be used. Breastplate and martingale are now optional. Saddle cloths are not permitted. Girths may be leather or web, preferably the former, but if web, should be cleaned and pipe clayed. Girth guards must be in place over the buckles. A sandwich case must be carried attached to the saddle and must contain food. White-string rain gloves must be carried under the girth on either side of the saddle, palms up, fingers toward the front of the saddle, right glove on right side, left glove on left side.

When packing, allow at least two shirts for each day of the show, for they get very dirty very fast. Always bring two coats and two pairs of breeches in case you have to ride in the rain and get soaked. Always take along a raincoat and rubber boots no matter what the weather looks like. For morning classes ratcatcher is usually acceptable and preferable, except in the case of a stake class or appointments class which has been scheduled for morning. For afternoon classes in horsemanship or hunter divisions, formal attire should be worn, as well, of course, as for evening classes in all divisions. Open jumping classes do not call for such formal attire, but the important thing in all classes is to be well dressed. Always wear a tie, stock or scarf and a hat. Most shows will not allow you to enter the ring without these. Also, you must wear a coat unless the show committee has announced that, due to hot weather, shirt sleeves will be acceptable.

Take along an old set of clothes for schooling before the show and any stable work you may be doing.

Always look your very best at a show by having enough clothes with you to allow frequent changes. You should always be neat and clean.

SUMMARY

When you are entered in a show you must prepare for each class by testing yourself on its individual requirements. For jumping classes you must set up courses as similar as possible to those which you will encounter at the show. Practice mounting and dismounting and riding on a loose rein for hack classes. Practice figure eights and rail performances for horsemanship. School your horse to line up well for conformation classes. The more you school, the better prepared you are for the final test of the show. Prepare your horse by trimming and grooming him thoroughly. For vanning he should have thick bandages on his legs, a tail guard, a sheepskin covering for his halter noseband. All grooming equipment, feeding equipment, feed and medicines should be sent to the show with the horse. You should have all the personal equipment you will need for your various classes, allowing at least one change of clothing per day. All necessary tack plus spares should be sent along. You and your horse should look your very best throughout the show.

CHAPTER XII

At the Show

ARRIVE AT THE SHOW as early as possible, at least an hour before the first class. For a two-day show both you and your horse should arrive early the day before so that you can get all settled and school over the courses if possible.

You should reach the show grounds before your horse does so that you will have time to go to the show secretary to find out where your stabling is located, and when your van arrives direct it straight to your stable. If you are showing more than one horse you should have arranged for an extra stall which you can use as a tack room and as a place for your groom or grooms to set up their cots for sleeping. Stables which show extensively often have elaborate tack-room furnishings including wall hangings, tack racks, cots and folding chairs, a table, lamp, etc. If you do not have an extra stall you can keep your tack in your tack trunk, which should be kept locked, right outside your horse's stall.

When you see the show secretary about your stabling also check on where water is available and, if you need feed or bedding, where it can be found.

As soon as possible, put the bedding in the stall and set up the pails for water and grain by hooking them onto baling wire wrapped around the boards.

When your horse arrives, water him and take off his shipping bandages and walk him for ten or fifteen minutes, for he'll be a little wobbly after the van ride. After he has rested and has had some hay, put the tack on him and walk him around the show grounds, letting him get used to the strange surroundings, and then take him into the ring and give him some work. If the course is open to schooling, take him over it once. If it is not open to schooling, don't try to school over it at all — it isn't cricket. What you can and should do, however, is walk the entire course on foot so that you can get an idea of the footing and scrutinize each fence carefully so that you can figure out what panel to take. If one panel of a fence has a looser rail than the other, don't jump that panel, for the rail can come off more easily if you just rub it and count as a knockdown. If there is a snake fence, figure out which panel brings you into the next fence at the best angle. If the footing in front of one panel is bad, or rutted from use, take the panel with the smoothest footing. Watch for muddy spots, holes, or uneven footing so that you can avoid them. Be sure to stay between the marked flags, for going on the outside of one of them means elimination for going off course.

Unless the show committee has ruled that no schooling is to be done in the ring, it is perfectly all right to work in it or set up any course you want to school over, but there will be other people schooling, undoubtedly, and you must take care not to get in their way and to take up as little space as possible. Remember, your whole attitude toward your competitors and fellow exhibitors must be one of co-operation and good will throughout the show. This is what showing is based on.

THE SNAKE FENCE
This is made of natural rails, is ofen found on hunter courses.

'While you are schooling you must not be concerned with what your audience is thinking but only with what will improve your performance. School just as you would at home, because this is your last chance before you are being judged.

Before you leave the show grounds that afternoon you must tear the time sheet out of the prize list and mark each class you are in, clearly indicating what horse you are riding in it and any deviations in tack. This should be given to your groom or tacked up on your horse's stall so that your groom will know when you want what horse and what tack. You should also mark any strip classes so that your groom will know he must be up at the end of the course before the class is ended in order to take the tack off and rub the horse down before the judging of conformation. Whenever the schedule permits, your groom should be at the out-gate to take your horse from you, but if he has other horses to get ready you must co-operate by taking your own horse back to the stable.

You must also make sure that your groom has enough money for meals and knows where to get them and that he knows where he is billeted for the night. If meals aren't available on the show grounds or nearby, find out what the other grooms are doing and arrange for him to eat with them. Otherwise you must either provide transportation for him or bring him supper before you leave. You're responsible for having taken him away from home, so you're responsible that he is well taken care of as far as eating and sleeping are concerned. Usually they can take pretty good care of themselves, but always be sure that they have.

As soon as programs are available you must buy one for yourself and one for your groom. Find out what numbers you need, get them from the show secretary. Mark each horse's number with his name on the back, and mark your horsemanship number with your own name so that your groom will know which one you want for each class and each horse. *Don't* lose your number! Most shows won't allow you in the ring without your original number, and many require a deposit on the number when you get it. However, if you *should* lose your number, as you no doubt will at some point in your showing career, get hold of an unused number and with soft pencil or black crayon mark the number you need on the back. Then turn the wire hook around so it will hook onto your coat. Just be sure it is legible. And at the end of the show, be sure to return *all* numbers, for they cost money and it's a nuisance as well for the show to replace them for their next show.

If your exhibitor's pass has not been mailed to you prior to the show be sure to get it from the show secretary before you leave the show grounds. If it is a major show you will probably need a pass for your groom also. If it is a show like the Garden you will also receive from the show secretary a calendar marking special times for schooling, all classes, and all social events. You will also get any passes or tickets necessary for luncheons or social events.

For fun, you might as well wander around the show grounds and stables to see who is there that you know, and if there's a horse-show party the night before the show arrange to go to it. If not, arrange a group for dinner; you only see most of these people at shows, and it's good to be able to sit around and talk nothing but horses without boring anyone. But don't forget to get to bed at a decent hour because you have long strenuous days ahead of you, and you can't ride well when you're exhausted. Sometime just watch the performances at the big week-long shows and notice how they get progressively worse as the horses and the riders fall prey to fatigue.

On the day of the show arrive early enough to get your horse out for a warm-up — a good long walk, some trotting, and a short canter, and maybe pop over a fence or two. Be sure that all your tack is in perfect condition, that your horse is shining, and that you have all the clothes you will need for that day's classes. If you are riding in both hunter-seat and saddle-seat classes be sure you have all the elements of both habits either in your car or your tack room, since either one or the other will probably have to serve you as a dressing room. And don't forget to have your boot jack and boot hooks ready for those quick changes. Also have a boot-polishing rag about, for you should try to keep your boots clean and shined all day long. If the grass is wet in the morning, just wear a pair of rubbers over your boots until it dries.

Be near the in-gate about five minutes before the scheduled time for your class, but be ready to go as long as half an hour before the appointed time, for the show committee is permitted to advance a class by half an hour. They are not permitted to change the order of classes, however, without twelve hours' prior notice to exhibitors or written permission from each exhibitor. Don't ever be late. Many shows will only wait three minutes before closing the class to late exhibitors, especially in the case of a jump-off.

THE LIVERPOOL
Found on open-jumper courses. This consists of a small coop, water or blue oilcloth, and a brush.

When you see that the gate man is accepting numbers for order of entrance into a class, go up and give him your number. If you have several horses in one class, explain this to him so that he can give you time between horses lest you hold up the class. On the other hand, if you have only one horse and another exhibitor has several and wants to enter before you do, you should permit him to do so. Always be completely courteous about waiting for your turn, and never try to get ahead of someone else for no good reason other than your impatience. Another reason some-one else may want to get into the ring before you is that he may have a horse who gets excited and unruly at the in-gate, as many do, and if he has to wait it may endanger those who are waiting at the in-gate. Let him go ahead, for someday you may be in the same position. Remember, there is no advantage to going in first, middle or last, and patience in waiting for your turn will be appreciated.

While you are at the in-gate awaiting your turn you should be watching other performances, particularly in horsemanship classes where you might be asked to change horses. You should also be watching the course, if it is unusual, so that you will be sure to know where you are going. Riding off course automatically means elimination.

When you enter the ring for your performance over jumps either in a hunter class, open jumping, or hunting-seat horsemanship class, it is customary to make one circle before heading into the fences. Make this at a trot, breaking into the correct lead as you come back to the rail, and proceed over the fences. Keep your pace even throughout the course, as a change of pace will count against you, except in open jumping, where only forward motion is required. If you have a refusal or runout, bring your horse back immediately to the fence where he had the runout, or in the case of a refusal, punish him with a good boot in the ribs or a slap with your crop, turn and walk back only a few steps, and take the fence. The further back you take him the longer he will have to think about quitting again.

When you have finished the course, stop your horse smoothly at the end of the ring and make a half circle at a walk or trot and leave by the out-gate. Don't stand at the out-gate; move away immediately to make room for the next horse. And don't take this opportunity to show your displeasure with your horse. If his perform-ance was not good, it's your own fault for not riding him well. And even if it had been his fault, punishing him now for something he did in the ring wouldn't do any good at all, for he can't know what you're thinking. If you had runouts or refusals, take him into the schooling ring, let him do it again, and *then* punish him, so he'll know what he's being punished for. If you've ever seen anyone lose his temper at his horse, at the out-gate or anywhere else, you know how it looks and how much good it does, and that should be enough to prevent you from doing it. Any time you lose your temper with a horse you're admitting defeat and might as well give up and go home.

Whenever you're in a walk, trot and canter class, just ride your own horse and stay as far away from everyone else as possible. Don't bunch up with the other horses at one end of the ring, and don't ever ride right next to someone — either make a circle or cut across the ring. If someone is riding right along with you, between you and the judge, either speed up and get ahead or slow down and cut away. If, however, you find yourself on the wrong lead at a canter, find an obscure corner of the ring, preferably on the outside of other horses so the judge can't very well see you, and stop immediately and change leads.

THE CHICKEN COOP
Usually painted white or red. Found on most hunter courses.

When you are asked to walk after a trot, the next command will probably be to canter, so prepare for it. Walk your horse out from the rail a few feet so that you can turn him in slightly when you break him, just to be sure he takes the correct lead. Also try not to be on any other horse's tail, for if the horse in front of you doesn't break immediately, you will be held up. As you break into a canter or while you are trotting or cantering, try not to cut anyone off, certainly not deliberately, for it simply isn't fair. Tricks like cutting off your competitor or hemming him in are not sporting, and showing *is* a game, not a business.

In a hack class you want your horse to go on a fairly loose rein, but if he will not, try to use only the rein on the outside, away from the judge, to slow him down while the inside rein is left loose. If he wants to keep a faster pace than you desire, keep him on the inside of the ring, not out on the rail, for this will make his turns sharper and this will slow him down somewhat. Remember, though, your trot should be fast and bold, without breaking, while your canter should be slow and collected, but still on a loose rein. When you are asked to hand gallop, do not race! Be careful not to get in a nose to nose competition with another exhibitor, and be sure to slow down almost to a canter on the corners. When asked to walk, stop your horse immediately and get the calmest, most flat-footed walk you can — no jiggling or jogging.

A hunting term which is often used by the ringmaster in the show ring is "hold hard," which means pull up, or stop. In the hunt field, this is a command from the huntsman to the field warning them not to override the hounds. In the show ring it may be used in a hack class to indicate everyone is to stop completely, such as after a gallop, or in hunter, jumper or horsemanship classes when a knocked down fence has not been righted in time for the horse to jump it again. When you hear a "hold hard," stop first and then look to see what is wrong.

When the command is given in a walk, trot and canter class to line up, turn into the center of the ring from wherever you are and line up facing the ringmaster. If you have a horse who gets herd-bound easily and won't leave the other horses, try to line up at one end of the ring, as far as possible from the next horse in line, taking your chances of being the first to be asked to make an individual performance. While you are lined up watch carefully every other performance. If you see the judge asking people to back their horses, one by one, prepare your horse to back, by collecting him, so that you will be ready to do it smoothly when your turn comes.

In a hunter class, if you are under consideration for a ribbon, you will be asked by the judge to trot up to a certain point and back again. When you do this, be sure not to look at your horse, particularly if he balks at moving forward. Never look at a horse who won't move forward, for he will think you are coming toward him, not going away from him, and surely won't move. Just cluck to him and start moving forward at a slight trot, and he will probably follow. If he doesn't, the ringmaster or your groom can wave his hand at him from behind or slap him on his rump and he'll trot out. When he does go, you should trot as fast as you can so that your horse will really trot out, not just dog along. If your horse should be going a little sore or lame in one foot, turn him so that the lame foot is on the outside of the turn, and be very careful to stop him before turning. Even a sound horse can look ouchy on a sharp turn at a trot, so be sure to walk around the turn before trotting back toward the judge.

As for your attitude toward the judges and other officials of the show, it should be one of utmost respect. They are the people on whom the show's very existence depends and should be treated accordingly. Under the rules of the AHSA no judge is required to explain his decisions to an exhibitor. As an exhibitor, you may, in an attitude of humility and respect, ask a judge what faults he found in your performance, and if he so wishes, he may explain them to you. As a rule, a judge is glad to do so, when courteously asked, for he is anxious to help where he may. Under no circumstances has an exhibitor the right to inspect the judge's card, though he may ask the show committee the reasons for any decision, and the committee, at their discretion may require the judge to give his reasons for the decision in question. A judge is never to be approached concerning any decision while he is judging or about to judge.

No exhibitor or employees or relatives thereof shall commit any act of discourtesy or disobedience toward any judge or official of the show or of the Association, and any such act shall be considered a violation liable to penalty by the Association. This includes any remark made during the show which might be considered offensive or intended to influence or cast aspersions upon the judging. Penalties include censure, suspension or expulsion from showing, forfeiture of winnings or a combination of any of these. These rules exist in the best interests of showing and of the people involved therein.

If an exhibitor, however, is aware of a specific violation of a rule or condition of a class, and is ready to substantiate such a claim by his testimony, he may make a protest. This protest must be signed by the exhibitor, and must be given to the show secretary along with a deposit of twenty-five dollars. If after a hearing of the show committee the protest is sustained, the deposit is returned to the protestor; if it is not sustained, the deposit is forfeited to the show. Generally, protests are to be avoided because they are a mark of poor sportsmanship as they are seldom valid. If, however, you are sure of a violation by another exhibitor, and this violation directly affects you, you are perfectly free to protest under the above conditions. But be sure of your ground before you speak. Protests are possible not only to avoid unfairness, but also to squelch unreasonable griping. If you've been around many shows you've undoubtedly heard an exhibitor say about a decision, "That isn't fair!" though perhaps not in so many words, and someone else answer, "Got twenty-five bucks?"

Your care of your horse all through the show should be the best possible. Keep his feeding schedule as close to normal as your showing schedule will allow. Be sure he is untacked between classes whenever there is enough time, and never put him in his stall when he is hot from a class. Rub him down and walk him until he is cool. If there is any breeze blowing put a cooler on while he is hot. If the air is chilly, keep a cooler on him even while you are waiting at the in-gate for your turn. Put the cooler over his rump and over part of the saddle so that you can keep it on him by sitting on it, and then put the cooler on again as soon as you come out of the class. In hot weather, sponge and scrape his back after every class, and keep his back perfectly clean throughout the show. Brush him off and clean his feet every time you take him out for a class. Keep his tail brushed and combed all day, and if any braids come out of his mane, be sure to rebraid them immediately. Any time you have to keep him out in the rain, put his raincoat or cooler on him so he and his tack won't get wet. If you are at a show like the Garden, where exercising can be done only at a specified time early in the morning, be sure to pull yourself out of bed in time to exercise your horse, no matter how late you were up the night before. Your horse must be worked each morning, and whenever possible he should be warmed up before his class. His performance will be the better for it.

And speaking of getting to bed late at night, many shows, particularly the larger ones, have quite a round of parties for their exhibitors, and since these are arranged for your pleasure, you should attend as many as you can. You'll find you'll have a lot of fun, though it may take great effort to get there after a tiring day of riding, and you'll meet a lot of amusing people and have a chance to talk to many of the people you haven't seen in some time, for you get little chance to talk to them during the busy day. You also get a chance to chat with the show officials, but please don't take this opportunity to drag an unsuspecting judge off into a corner to lecture him about the merits of your horse. Most judges will react unfavorably to this treatment and, while they may have listened patiently to your dissertation, when they see you in the ring they will probably lean over backwards in their efforts to favor no one in particular. If you actually want to talk to a judge about your horse or get his opinion, wait until the last championship ribbon has been pinned before approaching him. No judge likes to feel he is being forced into pinning any one horse. Nor is this the auspicious time to ask a judge why he didn't pin your horse in a certain class, for having watched hundreds of performances during the day, he is not likely to remember your horse unless his performance was outstandingly good or outstandingly bad, so you can't win.

THE TRIPLE BAR
Three single rails. Found on open-jumper courses.

At every show there is at least one representative of the press and at least one photographer, and at larger shows, there is a complete set of each. It is the job of each newspaper and magazine representative to get the best and most interesting story he can for his readers, and each will be looking for a different angle. Local papers are looking for stories about local people, and the top winners may be only of secondary importance to them, while large papers and national magazines are looking for the most unusual or biggest stories. So, you or your horse may be of interest to one of these people, in which case you will be approached by someone equipped with pad and pencil and a complete set of questions. Your reaction should be one of pleasure, not annoyance, and your answers should be perfectly honest. On the other hand, don't let the thought of your name in print fill you with conceit, for their interest in you is no measure of your skill. Your attitude should be one of co-operation, you should answer their questions truthfully and give them any additional information that you think might be of use to them. If they want pictures, let them take them. The call of press or photographer appeals to most people's vanity, but there are many who find it a bore and a nuisance, and if you are one of the latter, try to realize that you are momentarily public domain, and that good publicity never hurt anyone. Unfavorable publicity, however, is distasteful, so take care that you do not at any time deserve an unpleasant write-up, either by your actions, arbitrary attitude, or lack of sportsmanship.

If, however, you are in an important open jumping class indoors, where a flash bulb might hinder your horse's performance, you are, of course, perfectly free to request that no photographs be taken while you are in the ring. The blinding flash of light could disconcert your horse sufficiently to cause a hind rub or knockdown, but at outdoor shows where no flash bulb is necessary, there is little hazard of the photographer's presence near the fence causing any difficulty.

There are horse magazines with sizable circulations which, for a price, will publish the picture of a horse or rider on their covers or inside pages, and there have been cases where the parents of children in horsemanship classes have waged full-scale publicity campaigns in order to insure their children's success in showing. Many neophytes fall prey to this activity and should be warned against it. Rather than help a child, such a campaign is more likely, through its brazenness, to cause both judges and exhibitors to become hostile toward its subject, with unpleasant results. The zeal of horsemanship parents is often dangerous.

SUMMARY

Reach the show grounds early, before your horse, and find out where everything is so things can be ready for him when he arrives. Walk him around the grounds till he becomes accustomed to the strange surroundings. You should walk the course on foot to check paneling and footing. The amount of schooling allowed varies with individual shows. Mark your classes on a time sheet for your groom so he can have things ready always. Also, see that he has a place to sleep and to eat. Mark each number with the horse's name or your own. Warm up your horse before his first class. Be courteous at the in-gate. Watch other performances. Keep an even pace in the ring, stop smoothly and exit quietly. Your attitude toward all show officials must be one of courtesy and respect. Make a protest only when it directly affects you and when you are quite sure you are right. Take the best possible care of your horse throughout the show. Above all, be a good sport.

CHAPTER XIII

After the Show

WHEN YOU HAVE FINISHED RIDING in your last class of the show, and you are sure you have no chance for the championship and will not be called for a championship preliminary, you may prepare yourself and your horse for the trip home. If there is any possibility, however, that you may have to appear in a preliminary or championship class, you will have to wait until after such class before getting ready to leave.

You must be as careful getting ready to ship your horse home as you were in preparing him for the trip to the show. You should take the braids out of his mane and tail before leaving the show if you have time, for if braids are left in for any length of time, the hair will become brittle and break off, and your horse's mane and tail will start to itch from having had the braids in so long and he will start rubbing both against his stall boards or anything rough he can find. Groom him thoroughly and rub his legs with liniment diluted into a leg wash, and then bandage him with sheet cotton and shipping bandages, just as you did before the show, being careful that the bandages are snug enough to stay on, but never actually tight, for this will hurt the tendons and make them very sore.

If you are shipping your horse at night, remember to put plenty of warm clothes on him for the trip, for it may get very chilly. Also, be sure to put a tail guard or tail bandage on, and the sheepskin or bandage on the halter noseband.

Then gather up all your equipment and tack, clean it all as well as possible, and pack it neatly in your trunk. Check to see that you are going home with everything you brought, nothing less, and nothing more. If you have borrowed anything at all from any other exhibitor during the show, be sure to return it before you leave. And if you have lent anything to anyone, be sure that you get it before leaving. Empty and wash out your pails, take down any wires you left up around the stall, and leave things as neat as they were when you arrived. Take home any feed or bedding that is left over from what you brought.

According to the number of horses you had at the show and the length of the show, you should tip your groom. The usual amount is about five dollars per horse per day of the show, so for two horses at a two day show he would deserve twenty dollars. If you have won a reserve championship, you should give him an additional five or ten dollars, and if you have won a championship, give him an additional ten or fifteen dollars. This is customary procedure and is also a good investment if you value your groom's services.

If you have had an amateur riding your horse in a class or more, you should send him some small gift to show your appreciation, since he is not allowed to accept any real payment for riding. If you have one particular amateur who rides your horse for you at various shows, the customary practice is to give him one present at Christmas time, so that there can be no reflection on his status as an amateur.

Stay with your horse until the van comes for him and help the van driver and your groom to load him onto the van. Very bad accidents can occur in loading, particularly if it is not done with care and skill, and if there should be an accident, it is well for the owner to be there. One year at the Garden there was a very tragic accident in which a handsome three-year-old slipped off the ramp of the van onto the concrete and broke his leg. Since it was well after the show had finished for the night, the owner had left the premises, and it was a matter of hours before he could be reached. Meanwhile, the horse stood in agony, the vet waiting to do what was necessary but needing the owner's permission.

When the van leaves, you should leave for home, so that you will be at the barn before it arrives. When it does, your horse and your belongings should be removed promptly, leaving the van free to go on. Give your horse plenty of water, bed him down well for the night, and give him a bran mash. If he has already had his dinner, make the mash of bran only and don't give him too much. If your horse has not had dinner, make the mash of bran and grain and give him plenty of it. If it's cold out, you should make the mash of very hot water, putting a cloth over the top of the pail to steam it until it's cool enough for your horse to eat.

Your horse should not be worked the next day, but he should be walked for about half an hour if you have the time to do so, and even the day after that his work should be pretty light. This gives him a well-deserved rest after the hard work and tension of showing and puts him in good condition.

Now that the show is all over and you are home again, safe and sound, you should look over the events of the show and see just what you got out of it. Even if you won nothing at all, you certainly should have gained a great deal from the experience.

First of all, you should have learned about sportsmanship in action, having witnessed it in varying degrees in the varied and sundry group of people at the show. The importance of a complete lack of pettiness, of loving and understanding the sport, your competitors and your animal; the unpleasantness of cutthroat competition, of vicious striving for victory; the ugliness of poor sportsmanship as seen in the form of a rider beating his horse or neglecting him as retribution for a poor performance; the futility of pointless griping about the judging or conditions of the show; the foolishness of an exhibitor who sends his horse home after a few unsuccessful classes — these are some of the things you should have learned.

Secondly, you should have learned something about showmanship. The importance of being able to ride well under pressure and in competition; the ability to emphasize your best qualities and minimize your faults; the impression made by a confident rider trotting boldly into the ring for a class; the folly of being timid in the show ring; the worth of being a good competitor — these are what you should have learned about showmanship.

A good competitor, in showing as well as in other sports, is one who performs well under any circumstances, regardless of any of the various factors affecting his performance. This means that whether the ground was hard or muddy, whether it was rainy or hot, whether he felt ill or well, his performance was still his best, and he need not rely on any excuse such as these. If his performance was not good, he will admit that the fault was only in his riding. A good competitor is consistent. When you see him go into the ring you know you can expect a nice, steady performance. You know he won't lose the course, jab his horse's mouth, lose his pace, run through fences, or any of the many things you see in the show ring. A good competitor does not find fault with the judging. *Good* riders don't *need* excuses.

Furthermore, a good competitor seeks to help others, riders who may not have the same nerve and experience. If he is asked how the footing is on a course he gives an honest answer and tells about the slippery spot which might have ruined his own performance. He is never worried that he may be beaten by the help he has given another rider. He has enough confidence in his own ability to allow him to give help to the greener riders who need it for their very safety.

The point is that you want to have a foeman worthy of your steel. It's no fun to win in poor company — you want to have keen competition so your win is really worth something. It's like taking a top show horse to a little local show — you win everything because you've simply outclassed the other horses, and there's no sport in that. That's why people go to national horse shows — they want the strongest competition they can find. If you're really good, you'll win anywhere, and if you're not, you'll only improve by having the constant challenge of the best competition. Anyone who enjoys winning in poor competition is as poor a sport as someone who won't show in good competition for fear he'll be beaten. I have a few fifth and sixth ribbons which I value more highly than many blues — I know they were more honestly earned.

Just as race-horse breeders must strive constantly to produce horses with more and more speed, we must strive to improve the general standard of horses and riders for showing. The better the competition, the greater the challenge, making it necessary for each individual to improve himself and his horse constantly. We want the standard to be higher and higher so that there is real competition to make the sport more exciting. Poor performances are dangerous performances, so improvement lessens the hazard.

If you were really nervous before you went to your first show, you probably learned after a class or two that there really wasn't anything to be afraid of at all. If you didn't learn it, you had better learn it now. When fright seizes a rider, only the worst possible performance can ensue. The minute you get nervous, all those muscles which must be so flexible tighten up and refuse to function properly. Your hands get tense and irritate your horse's mouth, your back stiffens and you bounce around in the saddle instead of swinging with your horse, your legs stick out like spikes and you can't even keep them in place, much less use them. Many ordinarily good riders seem to fall apart when they get to a show, and ride miserably. Usually they relax a little after they've been to enough shows, but it's pretty grim until they do. You must forget that anyone is watching you and just do the best job you can.

If you feel a few butterflies fluttering around in your stomach just before you go into the ring, don't worry — that's all right. If you are just nervous enough to feel keen, you'll probably ride better. The butterflies will disappear the minute you enter that ring, and you'll ride better than ever. I used to worry when I wasn't just a little nervous because I wouldn't feel that spirit of competition, and I'd turn in a pretty mediocre performance, but when I had those butterflies I'd try harder and do better. If you are overconfident, you won't try hard enough to do a good job, but if you are overnervous, you will try too hard, which usually has disastrous results.

There is an old saying: "Good school, bad show," which means two things. It means that if you school well before the show, you will be overconfident in the ring, remembering your good performance before the show, and you won't ride well enough to get as good a performance this time. It also points out that a rider who can do a good job schooling and *is* a good rider simply may not ride well under pressure and will, therefore, not do a good job in the show. Some people, on the other hand, will school miserably and yet, when they get in the show ring, ride twice as well as they do ordinarily — they are just naturally competitive. As you get used to showing, however, you will probably learn very quickly how to compete well — it isn't hard.

And now, though you have come home defeated from your first show, you find you have actually triumphed. The day you go to your instructor for your first lesson after the show, apologizing for having done a bad job, you find he has a surprise for you. Conspicuously without ceremony he hands you two shiny new spurs.

WINNING YOUR SPURS

SUMMARY

If you are sure that you are not eligible for any championship classes you may prepare to leave the show early. Bandage your horse carefully and ready him for shipping. Be sure to take the braids out of his mane and tail. Gather all your equipment, clean your tack, return anything you have borrowed. Your groom should be tipped according to the number of horses and length of the show, with additional remuneration for any championship ribbons you have won. You should be there to help load the horse onto the van, and at the stable when he arrives. Give him a bran mash, and the next day let him rest, except for walking. Review what you have seen and heard at the show — what sportsmanship is, what competition should be, what showmanship is. A good competitor is a good sportsman, a steady performer, and a help to others. You should constantly seek better competition so that you will improve to meet it. Learn to be a competitive rider by overcoming excess nervousness. When you have learned all these things, you have earned your spurs.

Glossary

AGED: A horse over ten years of age.

AHSA: American Horse Shows Association. *See also* MEDAL CLASS.

AIDS: The rider's means of controlling and guiding his horse.

AMATEUR: One who receives no compensation for his activities in the sport.

APPOINTMENTS: Special articles of clothing, tack and equipment which must be worn in certain classes requiring hunt livery.

ASPCA: American Society for the Prevention of Cruelty to Animals. *See also* MACLAY.

ASSOCIATION, THE: AHSA.

BIT: The metal part of the bridle, which goes into the horse's mouth and which is what controls him when pressure is applied to the reins.

CANTER: A horse's gait to which the rider sits; similar to a gallop, but slower and more collected. *See also* LEADS.

CANTLE: The upward-curving back of the saddle.

CAST: When a horse has lain down in his stall, wedging himself against the wall so that he is unable to get up.

CHAMPIONSHIP: The highest award given in a particular division at a horse show; Reserve Championship is second to this.

COLIC: A severe stomach-ache in a horse caused by his having swallowed something indigestible.

COLLECTION: When a horse is driven up on the bit, flexing his head and neck, his stride shortened and in perfect cadence.

CONTACT: When there is no slack in the reins the rider is said to have contact with his horse's mouth.

CORINTHIAN: A hunter class in horse shows in which all riders must be amateur members of a hunt and must ride in hunting attire. *See also* APPOINTMENTS.

CROPPER: A fall of horse and/or rider.

CURB: A type of bit.

DAISY CUTTER: A good mover; a horse who moves close to the ground.

DIAGONALS: Since the trot is a diagonal gait, *i.e.* the horse's right hind and left front legs move together, the rider must post on one diagonal or the other, coming down in the saddle when either the right or left front foot of the horse is on the ground.

DISCONNECTED: Moving in long strides, out of cadence and uncollected; unco-ordinated.

DOUBLE: A type of bit combining snaffle and curb.

EXTENDED: Moving in long strides but in perfect cadence and with great spring and rhythm. At the extended trot the horse's toe hits the ground forward of his nose. *See also* COLLECTION.

FIELD: The body of the members of the hunt, following the hounds but remaining well behind them.

GLOSSARY

FLEXION: The arching of a horse's neck bringing the chin toward his chest, making the bit more effective in his mouth. Direct flexion is done with both reins; lateral flexion is done with only one rein, as in a circle.

FLOATING OF TEETH: The filing down of the sharp points of horses' molars which prevent them from chewing their food properly and discourage them from eating.

FLYING CHANGE: A change of leads at the canter in air, without stopping.

FOREHAND: The front legs and shoulders of the horse.

FROG: The sensitive triangular cushion on the inside of the horse's foot.

GALLOP: The fastest of the horse's gaits; an extended canter.

GIMPY: Showing lameness by favoring one leg.

GOOD HANDS CLASS: Special saddle-seat equitation class sponsored by the NHSA, the champion being chosen at the National Horse Show in New York.

GOOD KEEPER, or EASY KEEPER: A horse who eats well and is easily kept in good condition without a great deal of care.

GRASS CUTTER: *See* DAISY CUTTER.

GREEN: Without experience or knowledge.

GROOM (*v.*): To clean a horse.

GROOM (*n.*): Man who grooms; hence, stableman.

HACKAMORE: A type of bridle which cuts off horse's wind.

HALTER: A simple leather headpiece, similar to a bridle, which is used for leading or tying the horse in the barn.

HAND GALLOP: An extended canter, not as fast as a full gallop.

HAUNCHES: Rump and hind legs of a horse; hindquarters.

HEAVYWEIGHT: Hunter capable of carrying up to 205 pounds.

HERD-BOUND: Refusing to leave a group of horses and, once having left them, attempting to return to them.

HERRING-GUTTED: A horse who is particularly narrow at the point between his ribs and his hips.

HINDQUARTERS: *See* HAUNCHES.

HUNT CAP: Velvet-covered hard hat with visor, cork-lined; should be black, with ribbons turned up for an amateur.

KNOCKDOWN: In open jumping when a horse lowers the height of the obstacle it counts as a front or hind knockdown.

LEADS: At a canter, when a horse puts his left foot forward first, he is on the left lead; when he puts his right foot forward first, he is on the right lead.

LIGHTWEIGHT: Hunter capable of carrying up to 165 pounds.

MACLAY: Hunting-seat horsemanship class sponsored by the ASPCA, the champion being chosen at the National Horse Show.

MADISON SQUARE GARDEN: Scene of the National Horse Show in New York the first week of November every year.

MASTER (MFH): The Master of Foxhounds of a hunt.

MEDAL CLASS: Competition sponsored by AHSA for three seats of horsemanship in separate divisions: Saddle Seat, Hunting Seat, Stock Saddle Seat; the national championship for each is pinned annually by the AHSA.

GLOSSARY

MIDDLEWEIGHT: Hunter capable of carrying up to 185 pounds.

MOUTHING: Teaching a horse to move the bit around in his mouth, keeping his mouth moist, so the bit will be more effective; not fighting the bit.

MUSCLE UP: Getting a horse in good condition for racing, hunting or showing; turning fat into muscle.

NATIONAL HORSE SHOW: Scene of finals for Good Hands and Maclay.

NHSA: National Horse Show Association. *See also* GOOD HANDS.

OUCHY: A horse who seems afraid to put his feet down due to lameness.

PACK: A pack of hounds for foxhunting.

PELHAM: A type of bit.

PHA: Professional Horseman's Association.

POMMEL: Front part of saddle; on side saddle, two protruding horns on side.

POOR: A horse who is thin and in bad condition.

PORT: The bar of the Pelham or curb which is actually in the horse's mouth.

POST: To rise from and sink into the saddle at the trot.

QUALIFIED: Hunter who has a certificate attesting that he has hunted satisfactorily for at least one season with a recognized or registered pack.

RATCATCHER: Informal riding habit.

RECOGNIZED SHOW: A horse show licensed by the AHSA.

REFUSAL: When a horse refuses to jump a fence; three of these eliminate horse from a horse-show class.

RUNOUT: When a horse refuses to jump by running to one side of the fence; these are counted as refusals in scoring in the show ring.

SANDWICH CASE: Leather case carried on the side of the saddle behind the rider's leg; contains food and sometimes flask for nourishment while hunting; required in appointments classes.

SCHOOLING: Teaching a horse to do something; practicing.

SHAD BELLY: A formal black swallowtail coat for showing or hunting.

SHYING: When a horse jumps sideways from something which frightens him.

SNAFFLE: A type of bit.

SORE: A horse who is slightly lame.

SOUR: A horse who has had too much schooling, too much abuse, or too much jumping will become sour and oppose the rider's commands.

STOCK: Length of material which is tied around rider's neck.

STOCK UP: When a horse's legs or ankles, usually the hind ones, become swollen with lymph indicating a need of exercise or kidney trouble; when only one leg is stocked up it is usually from an injury.

STRIP CLASS: Conformation hunter class in which horses must be stripped of their saddles for the judging of conformation.

TACK (*v.*): To put the horse's tack on him, hence, to saddle and bridle him.

TACK (*n.*): All equipment used on a horse for riding.

TOUCH AND OUT: An open jumping class in which a horse is eliminated when he touches an obstacle. When there are no clean rounds the horses clearing the most obstacles win.

GLOSSARY

TUCKED UP: When a horse's flesh is drawn in at the point between his ribs and his hips from lack of food or water, or on account of illness; he appears herring gutted.

TURN A HAIR: To sweat, causing hairs of coat to turn upwards.

WEASEL BELLY: A formal black cutaway coat for showing or hunting.

WHIPPER-IN (WHIP): A member of the hunt staff whose job it is to keep the pack together by calling or snapping his whip.

Index

INDEX

INDEX

INDEX

INDEX

INDEX

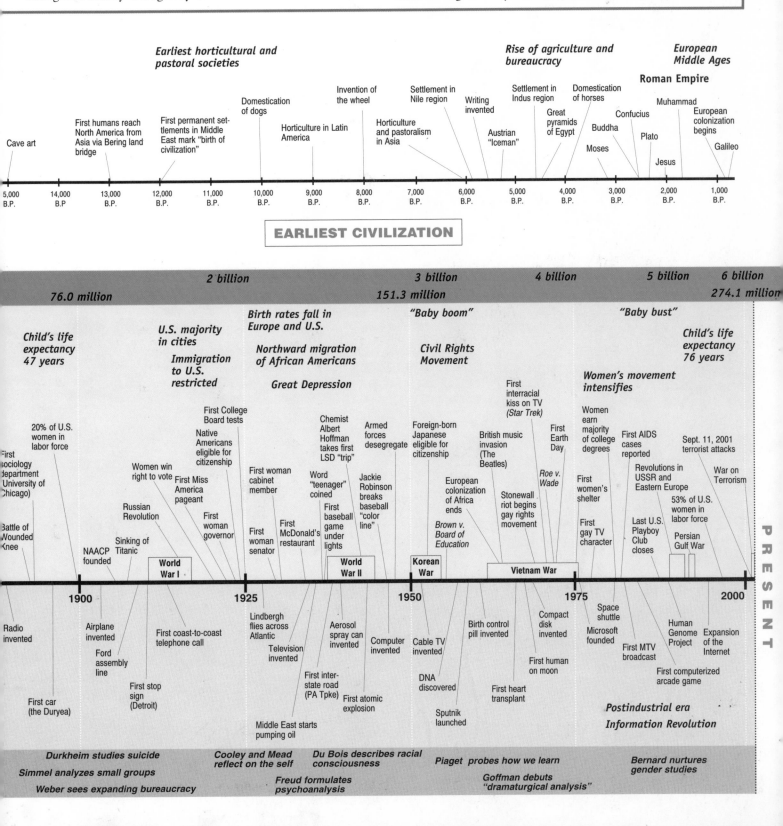

what we call civilization is relatively recent indeed, with the first permanent settlements occurring in the Middle East a scant 12,000 years ago. But the written record of our species' existence extends back only half this long, to the time humans invented writing and first farmed with animal-driven plows some 5,000 years B.P.

Sociology came into being in the wake of the many changes to society wrought by the Industrial Revolution over the last few centuries—just the blink of an eye in evolutionary perspective. The lower time line provides a close-up look at the events and trends that have defined The Modern Era, most of which are discussed in this text. Innovations in technology are charted in the beige panel below the line and provide a useful backdrop for viewing the milestones of social progress highlighted in the blue panel above the line. Major contributions to the development of sociological thought are traced along the very bottom of this time line.

Earliest horticultural and pastoral societies

Rise of agriculture and bureaucracy

European Middle Ages

Roman Empire

Cave art

First humans reach North America from Asia via Bering land bridge

First permanent settlements in Middle East mark "birth of civilization"

Domestication of dogs

Horticulture in Latin America

Invention of the wheel

Horticulture and pastoralism in Asia

Settlement in Nile region

Writing invented

Austrian "Iceman"

Settlement in Indus region

Great pyramids of Egypt

Domestication of horses

Moses

Buddha

Confucius

Plato

Jesus

Muhammad

European colonization begins

Galileo

| 5,000 B.P. | 14,000 B.P | 13,000 B.P. | 12,000 B.P. | 11,000 B.P. | 10,000 B.P. | 9,000 B.P. | 8,000 B.P. | 7,000 B.P. | 6,000 B.P. | 5,000 B.P. | 4,000 B.P. | 3,000 B.P. | 2,000 B.P. | 1,000 B.P. |

EARLIEST CIVILIZATION

2 billion   3 billion   4 billion   5 billion   6 billion

76.0 million   151.3 million   274.1 million

Birth rates fall in Europe and U.S.

"Baby boom"

"Baby bust"

U.S. majority in cities

Northward migration of African Americans

Civil Rights Movement

Immigration to U.S. restricted

Great Depression

Women's movement intensifies

Child's life expectancy 47 years

Child's life expectancy 76 years

First interracial kiss on TV (Star Trek)

First College Board tests

Native Americans eligible for citizenship

Chemist Albert Hoffman takes first LSD "trip"

Armed forces desegregate

Foreign-born Japanese eligible for citizenship

British music invasion (The Beatles)

First Earth Day

Women earn majority of college degrees

First AIDS cases reported

Sept. 11, 2001 terrorist attacks

20% of U.S. women in labor force

First sociology department University of Chicago)

Women win right to vote

First Miss America pageant

First woman cabinet member

Word "teenager" coined

Jackie Robinson breaks baseball "color line"

European colonization of Africa ends

Roe v. Wade

Revolutions in USSR and Eastern Europe

War on Terrorism

Russian Revolution

First woman governor

First woman senator

First McDonald's restaurant

First baseball game under lights

Stonewall riot begins gay rights movement

First women's shelter

Last U.S. Playboy Club closes

53% of U.S. women in labor force

Battle of Wounded Knee

NAACP founded

Sinking of Titanic

Brown v. Board of Education

First gay TV character

Persian Gulf War

World War I

World War II

Korean War

Vietnam War

| 1900 | 1925 | 1950 | 1975 | 2000 |

Radio invented

Airplane invented

Ford assembly line

Lindbergh flies across Atlantic

Aerosol spray can invented

Computer invented

Cable TV invented

Birth control pill invented

Compact disc invented

Space shuttle

Human Genome Project

Expansion of the Internet

First car (the Duryea)

First stop sign (Detroit)

First coast-to-coast telephone call

Television invented

First interstate road (PA Tpke)

DNA discovered

First human on moon

First heart transplant

Microsoft founded

First MTV broadcast

First computerized arcade game

Middle East starts pumping oil

First atomic explosion

Sputnik launched

Postindustrial era

Information Revolution

PRESENT

Durkheim studies suicide

Cooley and Mead reflect on the self

Du Bois describes racial consciousness

Piaget probes how we learn

Bernard nurtures gender studies

Simmel analyzes small groups

Freud formulates psychoanalysis

Goffman debuts "dramaturgical analysis"

Weber sees expanding bureaucracy